SECRETS OF

ETERNITY

By Annalee Skarin

DeVORSS & Co., *Publishers*
516 WEST NINTH STREET
LOS ANGELES 15, CALIFORNIA

© 1960

by

Annalee Skarin

Printed in the United States of America by—
DeVorss & Co., Publishers, 516 West Ninth St., Los Angeles, Calif.

SECRETS OF ETERNITY

FOREWORD

The past ages of eternity were forgotten in that moment when I was privileged, for the first time, to look down upon the earth. The joys, the achievements, the progress, the infinite happiness and the glory of perfection became factors of secondary importance. The one great, all-engrossing reality was the scene before me of a world so lost in darkness and so engulfed in error and filled with suffering I felt my heart would break. Compassion and love poured from me in overwhelming waves of tenderness as I beheld the earth. It was a world where the great Light had become submerged in an ignorance of blinding unbelief. And yet the Light was everywhere. The Light was the one great, eternal reality of infinite glory. Yet that Light had become buried in an ignorance of overwhelming digression as man had wandered from the TRUTH.

As I stood weeping over a world so filled with darkness, so lost in evils and so unaware of the Light, I was permitted to behold every human being upon it. I gazed upon the continents and beheld the nations, the cities, the hamlets and the far places where few human beings dwelt. I beheld the abodes of mankind and the individuals who inhabited them. And in their hearts and upon the whole earth was only the gloom of darkness—and the hand of death waiting for its victims.

It was as though the whole world was enfolded in a dim, gray veil of eternal twilight. It was a twilight in which no radiant sunset left its lingering glow of passing

9

beauty or its warm, caressing touch. That appalling gloom engulfed the entire planet and every human being upon it. The great eternal Light of Christ was uncomprehended simply because it had been rejected. Even the slightest knowledge of ITS great effulgence and ITS unutterable power was unknown.

When I could finally concentrate my energies to look beyond the darkness of that enfolding, somber veil, I beheld that every individual was wading in mud. And that mud was the sad result that had been created through each individual's actions and reactions to earth's conditions and to mortality. The more an individual clung to the gross, physical things of earth the more the mud clung to the individual. Some were only slightly soiled by it as their feet stepped lightly along the paths of earth. Their defilement was in a lesser degree.

There were others, however, who literally wallowed in the mire; and there were a few who were completely immersed in it. The muddy slime was smeared over their faces and in their hair and their fingers dripped with it. Of all the inhabitants of the earth there was not a single soul who was not, in some degree, struggling through the defiling influences of mortality. Both the mud and the darkness were conditions which had been created by man and had become so universally accepted they were taken for granted. They were conditions that were completely accepted and unchallenged.

The most tragic part was the knowledge that each individual was stirring up his own muck without realizing that he alone was responsible for his condition. It was heartbreaking to behold. The whole world was completely enslaved by the great ignorance. There was not a single soul upon the entire earth who had even the slightest idea of the Light of Christ, though It had been mentioned so many times in their inspired scriptures and through various revelations. All were so engrossed in the mud and the darkness they seemed to comprehend naught but the physical world and that which pertained to it.

Much of earth's energy was being directed to the invention of mechanical wonders and those mechanical wonders were claiming the rest of mankind's energy just to operate them. Each invention only increased the darkness and the fears, the errors and the evils and individual unprogressiveness as those same inventions took over the mind of man. Man's absorption in the inventions prevented him from making the great inner soul search so necessary for releasing the divine Christ Light. Each man carries that Light within himself—and knows it not. "The Light of Christ is given to abide in every man who cometh into the world." But because of the great ignorance, man walks in darkness and under condemnation.

As I watched the earth and poor struggling humanity, love poured out from me in overwhelming waves of sorrowing compassion. I would gladly have given my very existence—even my soul, to have in some way helped to reveal that divine Christ Light, and the source of it. In that great time, before the now, I comprehended fully the powers of that Light. I realized that Christ's Light alone could bring the great healing to a world so submerged in darkness and engulfed in suffering. I also comprehended and knew fully that the great Light was everywhere. I knew that It was concentrated in the soul of every man, awaiting only man's acceptance of It in order that It could be brought forth with Its unutterable powers.

Yes, the Light was everywhere. It was in all creation and all created things. It was given to abide in all men and in all realms and all kingdoms. There is no place in existence where His Light is not. It is even in the darkness, and the darkness comprehends it not. And though the Light is everywhere, the earth was seemingly a planet devoid of It for the simple reason that man did not comprehend the Light, and so rejected It because of the great ignorance of the ages. The world was entirely engulfed in the darkness because man was completely unaware of that divine Light which had been given to abide right within himself. Because of that rejection man was submerged in the gloominess and the negative conditions of earth. The sins and evils and heart-rending sorrows and sufferings of the ages became their mortal heritage.

As I lingered to behold the dusky obscurity and its consequent evils, I felt that I would melt in a compassion so tender and so intense it would consume me. My soul cried as it yearned in indescribable sorrow and infinite love. A burning desire to be permitted to go to earth to help reveal His Light filled my being.

"If only I could go down to a world so lost in darkness," I thought, as I lingered there in tender sorrow. "I could help man comprehend the Light. It would no longer be rejected and remain inactive and impotent in the lives of the children of men. I am sure I could help to make It manifest upon the earth. The great Light is everywhere! Only the earth is completely unaware of It! And because of their unawareness it is as though the Light were not.

"Oh, dear God, please have mercy upon the world! Have mercy, God!" I breathed.

As I thus stood in yearning, filled with infinite love, my

sorrow enfolded a world lost in darkness and despair. My sorrow seemed deeper than any sorrow ever known on earth. It seemed more intense and more heartbreaking. No earthly sorrow can outlive a lifetime and usually earth's sorrows are for but a few hours. Rarely are they for more than a few days, weeks or months. My sorrow enfolded a world and many, many lifetimes, for generation upon generation was involved—and every human being was enfolded in my yearning compassion. My grief encompassed the entire history of the earth and every individual upon it.

It was while I thus stood, yearning in tender compassion over a dark and dreary world, that a messenger of Light touched me gently and announced in awed love, "It is your turn to go to earth. I have come to summon you to the council chamber of God, that you might be sent direct from His throne."

There is no language, not even in heaven, to bespeak the glory surging in my heart and the joy that sang in my soul as I heard those endearing words. My request, though unspoken and unexpressed, was to be fulfilled! My desire to go to earth was granted! A reverence and devotion of almost overwhelming gratitude filled my being. Of all the joys of eternity that one alone lingers in my memory as the greatest.

———

I was ushered into a great hall of glory. The floors and walls were of precious stones, in which the life energies were plainly visible. The stones were alive! All stones are living, but in the world of Spirit that life is discernible and apparent. At the time I was neither impressed nor astonished at the splendor of that vibrating life. It was later in mortality, when I recalled the occasion, that I marveled over the ability to behold the living life essence in substance, especially in stones.

It was many years later, when I had finally comprehended the living vibrance of atoms and life's flowing essence of eternal spirit substance, that I also comprehended

that in the higher world one can behold the life energies in their true spirit form in all substance and in all things. But for many years that memory only filled me with a marveling awe and a deep wonder.

At the far end of the great, glorious room was a platform, a stage, or a raised area, with seven circular steps which led upward to that elevated summit. At the top was a glorified throne of vibrating light. Each step leading up to it was composed of a precious, living gem, in color like a rainbow hue. Each step was a blending color with the stone above and the stone below. Together they held the living radiance of the rainbow, revealed in its perfection as they displayed the life essence of the divine, spiritual substance of which they were composed.

I was neither interested in nor concerned with the precious jewels of living beauty, nor with the vastness of the room, nor in the throne of living Light. Christ was seated on that throne and He held all my attention and all the concentrated powers of my love and adoration centered in humble devotion.

As I beheld Him I went down upon my knees in loving gratitude and yielding reverence. Every fiber and cell of my entire being reached out in utter and complete surrender and in an adoration as alive and vibrant as my intelligence could offer. My gratitude for the privilege of being sent to earth was singing from my heart in a symphony of humble praise. My very devotion was so deep and intense and love-filled I wondered how I could ever rise to my feet and cross the intervening space to that great throne— where He sat waiting.

I still have no recollection of how I traversed the distance. I only recall kneeling upon the second or third step, bowed in humble adoration and infinite, overwhelming love.

And He called me by my name, the name that was given and reaffirmed at birth. "Annalee, you have been privileged to come here to make any request you may desire for your sojourn on earth. You may be born a princess and rule as a queen, if you so desire. You may have any or all of the talents you request. You may have wealth and honor, or any gift, or gifts, you wish."

I kneeled silent and still, unable to express the overwhelming yearning crying in my soul. I was choked with the burden of my request; it was so intense. How could I possibly express my overpowering desire? How would it be possible to explain that I desired no special position, no particular talents, no honors or wealth or physical gifts? How could I express the spiritual yearning that burned within my heart? The intense desire crying within seemed inexpressible. The yearning to be privileged to go to earth in the hope and the assured belief that I could help dispel the great ignorance and reveal the Christ Light because I comprehended it so well, was still beyond my power to utter. Speechless and dumb, I knelt in an intensity of longing too deep to express even in the world of Spirit.

The living essence of my unspoken prayer vibrated out and revealed itself as I could never have done. The Christ Light released within that longing in my soul made Its own petition known, expressing clearly the things I had no power to reveal.

And then He answered and His words were a song of utter glory vibrating through my soul. Softly, gently and with penetrating love, He said, "I understand your desire. It shall be granted. I am so pleased that this is your request. There have been others who have had similar desires. Fear not, you will accomplish much."

I looked up then, weeping for joy. He smiled and His love poured out in a glory that filled my heart and my soul and the vast, gorgeous room—and, I am sure, even the universe thrilled with it also.

So it was that I received my assignment and my ordination and was sent to earth with a destiny resting upon me that was far greater than I.

———

Needless to say, I was born without talents or wealth or position.

My infancy and childhood were spent in being thoroughly initiated into the mud in all its most earthly aspects of suffering, lack and its harsh unloveliness. The very darkness seemed to concentrate upon an effort to destroy me before my work was ever begun.

By the time I had reached fourteen there was little left of dreams or hope or joy or happiness. I hated life. I hated this world and everything upon it. And out of that ugliness a whisper arose from deep within that left a disturbing feeling that some day I was to write.

When I was sixteen, that dream seemed to clarify itself more substantially as it whispered a little louder of things that were meant to be; then for one moment, on a summer's day, I caught a glimpse of perfection. It was only a glimpse that thrilled and vibrated through my being in living ecstasies—and then was gone—driven out by discords, harshness and the ugliness of all existing things in my life scope.

It was only after I was mature and freed to think and feel for myself that the dream returned in tantalizing wisps, as I sought to find myself and know my own values and my own strength. Others had taken over my life so definitely from the beginning I had never been able to find out what my own inclinations were. There was always a wistful longing to know what I would do on my own, if only I had been given a chance to make a decision. I was more silently dismayed over never being permitted to "be me" than I was over the misery, the domineering and the continual, undeserved punishments.

Always, during the moments of deepest despair throughout my entire, desolate childhood, moments when it would otherwise have been utterly impossible to have gone on, I would recall a smile and remember that at some time in the past, Someone had loved me.

I was in my late twenties before that memory was restored in all its splendor. That memory was not given to me until I had found myself and chosen my own way. With the restoration of that pre-mortal memory came the sure knowledge that some day I was to write. And then it was that Satan came and offered me wealth and fame and a life of luxury if I would write as he directed. That was an awful moment in my life. Not that the offer even tempted me. I was outraged and indignant. It was Lucifer's overwhelming, overpowering personality that was so completely terrifying.

I was not sure I would not be completely destroyed by

giving my resolute answer in outward firmness and inward trembling as I said, "I would not write for you if you were to give me the whole world—and everything upon it. If I ever write it will have to be with a pen dipped in heaven. It will have to be for the glory of God and for the benefit of man."

In that instant he was gone and my prayer followed the expressing desire offered in that grim moment of inspiration, "Dear God, if I ever write, let me write with a pen dipped in heaven."

I am sure that Satan made his offer to others. It may not always have been as openly as was his approach to me. But in some way he held the promise of earthly honors, of wealth and fame dangling before the eyes of those who aspired to write. Hundreds gave heed to his offer, for from that time on the vile sex books of earthly degeneracy and grubbiness, along with the shocking books of crime and violence began to be not only accepted, but acclaimed. And a world sank into a deeper level of degeneracy than it had for many centuries. The darkness became greater, the mud deeper and the evil more intense. Virtue became a thing of mockery and soberness a subject of highest ridicule. Love almost seemed to vanish from the earth as mankind became more animal-like and seemingly lost the ability for natural affection. Only law still held, and it was something to be winked at. Many of the world's law-makers became conceited imbeciles, corrupted and unwise. Individualism, greatness and inspiration vanished in a "follow-the-leaders" game which led nowhere. And those who followed became insipid, unthinking robots with nothing but the ability to make a great noise that silenced individual progress.

Against such loud, mocking derision by the puppets of

evil, my voice would remain unheard if it were not for the strength of those who made the same request as I.

I am the least of them all—the weakest of the weak. But at last God has let me dip my pen in heaven and write the truths so necessary to help save a world from utter and complete destruction. That pen is dipped in love, the love of truth and light. I have written neither for money nor for fame. No royalties have been mine, no paid price accepted by me for any of my works.

My increasing love has been the reward for my efforts, for my love is great and my vision true. All that I have I give freely to the world. I seek no credits or rewards. I only ask that men read that which God has revealed through me in humble prayer. If man will but be as prayerful in reading as I have been filled with humble prayer in the writing, then there is still hope for the world.

And so, beloved ones of earth, I say, come stand with me upon the mountain top and permit me to show you the cause of the darkness that it might be dispelled. Let me lead you to the great Christ Light that you might step out into its glory and abide in the new day.

With compassionate love, unfeigned and true, I reach out to tear asunder the veil of the "Gross darkness that has covered the earth and blinded the minds of the people." With love and tenderness increased a thousand-fold, I will reveal first the weaknesses and the evils and the errors and deceits contained within the earthly mire that you might fully comprehend the issues involved and so step forth into His great Light, redeemed and glorified.

THE TRUTH BEHIND THOUGHT

Chapter I

If you have read the books preceding this one it will make this record more comprehensible and more easily assimilated. This is the record that holds the final map to the highway of glory.

When one reaches the higher altitudes in the journey of his upward climb, he leaves the old earth laws and ways behind. In order to abide permanently in that realm of high, singing, glorious vibration and eternal light, he must comprehend the issues that are involved. He must also understand the higher laws and be able to use them with power. The "righteousness of His kingdom" is a knowledge of the right-use of its laws.

Each individual will learn, in the upward ascent, that every negative thought and feeling becomes a weight upon his body and a drag upon his soul. Negative thoughts and feelings have power not only to retard one's progress but to stop it completely, unless overcome. Mortal thinking is mostly negative, discordant, selfish thinking. From here on the negatives must be completely understood. It is necessary to know that the negative thoughts and feelings contain all the laws of the lower realms of physical darkness. As long as an individual abides in the vibrations of negative thinking and negative feeling, he cannot possibly progress into the light or walk with power.

The laws of God, the laws of overcoming, the laws of

21

glory and happiness and power are contained in the ability to think truly. True thinking is the processing of one's thoughts as they are brought under control by complete comprehension of their purpose and power. True thinking is the thinking which holds the keys of faith-filled, magnificent, unspeakable joy that all so greatly desire. Many are deceived and enticed into evil dens and dives of iniquity, thinking that joy is obtainable by imbibing strong drinks. Too late they learn that "strong drink is a mocker". There are many who have to discover this truth for themselves. Few can be told. Any who become drinkers lose the power to think clearly and correctly. They not only relinquish their power of true thinking, but even their very freedom is confiscated in time.

As one progresses into the higher realms he must leave all negatives behind. One can neither think nor feel the discordant, harassed, evil things of which mortal life is composed. The point of transition is where one comprehends this fact and drops the negative aspects, knowing fully what he is doing and what he will accomplish.

True, divine thinking is always love-filled, joyous and free from all evil vibrations. In divine thinking there are no thoughts of evil, of lack, of fear or hate and distress. True thinking *is* divine thinking. True thinking is so love-filled that fear, darkness and all evil flee before it. "Perfect love casts out all fear."

Man's creative ability is contained completely in his thinking and feeling processes. Any thought, dropped into the emotions so it becomes something an individual actually *feels,* will become an established, definite reality in his life. Hate, envy, jealousy, joy and love are a few of the emotions which can be released as living vibrations of forceful reality as one actually *feels* them. All evil thoughts such as hate, anger or selfish thinking, when thus awakened in one's feelings, bring the conditions of old age, disease, poverty and all earthly misfortunes. All the negative aspects of life come to an individual as real experiences because of his own negative thinking, including the final seal of mortality, which seal is death.

Glorified, love-filled thoughts of praising gratitude awaken and bring forth the gifts and powers of life eternal. Behind every glorious, love-filled thought is contained the breath of everlasting life.

These truths have been more thoroughly explained in the books which preceded this one. These facts are only restated briefly to reveal for a moment the foundation on which truth rises.

Lie detectors reveal the facts behind what has just been stated. The most hardened criminal, the most adroit liar or the most composed villain is mentally, physically and emotionally jarred by every false statement he may chance to utter. No individual can ever become immune from the effects of any untruth he may speak, no matter how mild or seemingly inoffensive that lie may appear. The effects of a lie are registered in their disintegrating power upon every cell and fiber of his being. He can no more escape their results than he can fool the lie detector or change the pattern of his fingerprints. The instrument only registers those destructive vibrations as they work upon the man himself. The results of a lie are always just as definite whether the lie detector is used or not. The instrument only picks up those disintegrating reactions from the being of the transgressor. The machine is not creating those inharmonious markings that are so completely out of harmony with the individual's true pattern of rhythm.

It must be understood here that an individual's habit of falsifying is weaving the pattern of his own destruction. If one is not an habitual liar and only tells little white lies occasionally, he is still injuring himself. If he is telling great untruths to injure someone else, the most lasting results for evil will be upon himself, though he is the last person to suspect it.

This is not only true of a lie but it is true of every evil emotion or feeling, every habit and every discordant thought. It is the true reality behind thought.

He who cheats in any business or in any transaction whatsoever in dealing with his fellowmen is only cheating himself. No soul is immune from the shrivelling results to his own inner being as he cheats, on either measures or qualities or time.

Homosexuals, sexual perverts and such are carrying with them the most deadly of all destructive poisons. And they themselves are the ones who are partaking of the poison which is being produced right within themselves by their own negative, uncontrolled thoughts and habits. Any who create such poisons will drink fully of the bitterness they contain. Their first loss is the loss of their own self-respect, which is a priceless attribute. It is most difficult to replace. After the loss of self-respect there is little left to build upon. Only disintegrating decadence is left as they sink into the slime of repulsiveness and darkness. The only hope in existence for such as these is for them to comprehend the issues, then with increased understanding and almost super-human determination begin to battle for their release from enslavement and their rights to lost powers and lost virtues. Theirs is always the power to overcome, if so be they desire. Their very overcoming gives them power to rise triumphant forever.

Sex perversion is caused, in almost all cases, by uncontrolled thoughts. It is a condition that is self-encouraged and hence self-developed. When such uncontrolled thoughts and feelings are strong enough they become the controlling factors and the persons who created them become the slaves. Most over-sexed individuals have become so through their own thought processes. From their own minds and emotions have come the seeds of their downfall. In the emotions those seeds of thought were nurtured into feelings that went out of bounds. In such degeneracy it is possible for man to sink below the level of the beasts.

I regret that it is necessary to include this chapter and the one that is to follow. I promise you that some day they will both be dropped completely from this record. The time is coming when they will no longer be needed. They are included at the present time so the issues involved between light and darkness might be fully comprehended, and to fulfill the promise that: "All men might be left without excuse." It is the point of demarcation with which this work deals. This point must be clearly defined so that all may fully comprehend the issues involved and glimpse the glorified realms ahead. This is quite necessary in order that the transition might be made while still in mortality. In truth, it is the point where mortality can take on immortality through perfect understanding, divine obedience to truth and with great love. This is the point along that upward climb in which the laws and powers of eternity can become fully operative as one leaves the mortal realms. This is the point of egress from the earth plane onto the higher plane, where mortality takes on the properties of immortality. The dividing line is as sharp a line as is the River of Life to those who pass through the experience of death. None can possibly travel into the higher realms without comprehending in the fullest detail the issues involved. These first two chapters are written to indicate the ways of mortality that they might be forever left behind.

It is by vision that all things come forth. The power of vision is the power of creation. The power of vision is also the power or gift of imagination. It is the power to "image in" to the emotions one's thoughts until they become alive and active so they are registered as feelings or intense desires. It is then they will produce or bring forth the tangible results. This is the law which holds the everlasting powers of creation within its embrace. This knowledge reveals the true aspect of the "Tree of Good and Evil". This law of creation will as readily produce all good as it will evil. Within man himself is contained the seed of its fruitage. Man holds the keys and powers of all creation right within himself. Whether the results of such powers are good or evil is of man's choosing. "He has all that the Father has," even the full powers of creation. Man himself chooses how he will use such powers.

In the past these creative powers have been mostly misused through man's gross ignorance. It is time for that blinding veil of ignorance to be torn asunder and for man to begin to stand forth as a master and the deciding factor in such creative processes.

Man can sink below the level of the beasts simply because he has the ability to *think* below the level of an animal's thinking, if so be he uses his God-given powers in that manner. He may also become as God simply by learning to think as God thinks.

In the Sermon on the Mount is contained the key of this everlasting truth. The full idea is contained in a revelation of magnificent beauty. It admonishes one to be *willing* to go the second mile, or to go that second mile *willingly*. The first mile was all that was required. The second mile was a service rendered in complete willingness. It was an added offering that would have the power to dispel any vibration of resentment against that first, required mile. It instructs one in the forgiving love that requires him to pray for his enemies with a divine, loving compassion. He is instructed to do good to those who have rendered him evil, and to be willing to serve the least and most unworthy of all God's children. He is not only to pray for his enemies but to love them also, that he might "Be perfect, even as his Father in heaven is perfect."

This invitation to become perfect, even as the Father in heaven is perfect, contains the vision divine. It is a possibility and a promise as definite and real as the promised diploma is to the student who is working for it. God will not be mocked. Neither has He ever mocked His children by giving a promise that is impossible to fulfill. Every promise He ever gave must and will be fulfilled, whenever man has developed the faith to receive.

Following is the quotation from Mark Chapter 11, verses 24 and 25, as translated from the Latin Vulgate: "Therefore I say unto you, all things, whatsoever you ask when ye pray, believe that you shall receive; and they shall come unto you.

"And when you shall stand to pray, forgive, if you have

aught against any man; that your Father also, who is in heaven, may forgive you your sins."

It is by pure, high vision and earnest prayer that all existing evils, which have already been produced by man's erroneous thinking, can be overcome, transformed and converted into blessings. It is true that even one's evils and errors and mistakes can be transmuted into blessings in this manner. Let your regrets be turned into weapons of power as they are used as flaming swords to destroy the night.

Every thought that has been harbored in the emotions until it becomes a definite feeling or an urgent desire is a living power of intense vibration. Vibrations are the forces that can heal or destroy the earth, according to their source of release and the quality of their heritage. If they are vibrations sent out on the wings of love and light they hold the powers of infinite healing and of all good. If they are bred in evil thinking and negative emotions they can literally destroy the earth, and most assuredly will bring harm to him who created them.

Within man himself is contained all the powers of this reality of creation. Every thought that has developed into a feeling is a vibration. And every vibration will go forth to produce the tangible realities behind its spiritual thought form. Vibrations are the very life forces behind the tangible realities.

Many try to lift their vibrations by false prodding. This measure is very destructive. The only true power of exaltation, whether it be man himself, his thoughts or his vibrations, is contained in the eternal laws of right thinking and right emotions as one uses his God-given powers of creation correctly. All the efforts to climb into those higher vibrations by any other method than the true one will fail.

All the dives and dens of iniquity are gloomy, darkened, depressing sepulchers in which the lights of men are being extinguished. It is possible that they may be considered fashionable, extremely luxurious and very "smart" as they display their expensive furnishings. Nevertheless they are only for those who are satisfied with the counterfeit happiness, or for those who have trained themselves to abide in the darkness (of their own evil thinking), rather than in the light.

There are many who have become completely deceived by this shoddy sham, this false flicker that obscures their vision. He who needs to find his "Christmas cheer", or any other cheer for that matter, in a bottle is only snatching at false sunbeams which turn into shadows as he seeks to lay hold upon them. The glowing coals of promised warmth and beauty become only the cold, gray, burned-out ashes of regret in his hands. Those who drink to be sociable will find out sooner or later that they are left alone, forsaken by all.

Such false prodding, such counterfeit cheer, such vain "lifts" are the great deceits of the darkness. In such darkness one's own evils and lacks may be momentarily less noticeable.

Those who get a fragmentary, deceptive "lift" from any stimulant, liquor or drug, are but "Going up another way, and will be cast out". They are blindly seeking to lift their own low vibrations by a false method. They are tragically seeking to enter the kingdom of heaven by another road than the one Christ mapped.

The kingdom of heaven is a condition of high, glorious, vibrating light and power and eternal happiness and unspeakable, everlasting joy. This higher kingdom of exquisite, glorified vibrations of eternal light is the great reality. It is impossible for mortal man to conceive of the wonder and the glory of it, "for such has never entered into the heart of man", neither can the mind of man encompass it. It is into this realm that those who dissipate, even in the least degree, are seeking admittance and they know it not.

In attaining to this Kingdom through right thinking and right feeling, through love and praising adoration of true gratitude one obtains this kingdom of high vibrations as an everlasting possession. He needs no false paths of evil to make him *"think"* and *"feel"* that he is there, when he is only surrounded by darkness. Neither will those who go up the right way need to be "cast out" of its divine precincts. This true vibration of singing glory becomes the permanent condition of all who attain unto it by the proper method. This realm of Light becomes the abode of him who learns to love the Lord. It is his eternal heritage—*now* and forever.

Those who are satisfied with that false, momentary, deceptive "lift" have only the "letdown" awaiting them.

And every "letdown" is a little more violent than the "lift". Every one who goes up by any false method will be thrust out as violently as the stimulated vibration was evil. Always the "letdown" is as great or greater than the "lift" he received by his dissipation. "Get a lift from a cigarette" and get dropped just a trifle deeper each time. "Get a lift" or a "pickup" from any source, except by traveling "His Way", and your expulsion will be measured by the degree and intensity of the "lift". And after a while all false prodding and all stimulants lose their power to even give that imagined "lift".

All such "lifts" are only childish, make-believe, false

joys in an empty void of darkness. And each "lift" into those higher vibrations is but another link added to the chain that will eventually enslave the individual so he is no longer free. He still may prate about his "freedom" and discover, too late, that it is only "doom" he has paid for. Too late, he will realize even that "doom" was not "free", for he will have purchased it at the price of his own soul.

One of man's greatest "free" gifts is the God-given gift of *free-agency*. This divine gift is the one which the powers of darkness are seeking hardest and always to confiscate. When man loses his free-agency by becoming enslaved to sin, dissipation, vices, wrong thought patterns and vile habits, he does not realize until too late that he has cast away a priceless possession as a thing of little worth.

Man's right to choose the thoughts he thinks contains all the creative powers of eternity, even the creative powers of Godhood. If he uses these powers amiss or misuses the divine gift of free-choosing, he will lose his free-agency. It is in the loss of free-agency that one becomes enslaved by the powers of darkness. The great issues today are over this divine, God-given gift. All dictatorial governments must take away man's free-agency from him in order to obtain and hold their power. When this happens either politically or morally, man is no longer free. He is a slave.

Behind every thought and feeling are the vibrations of their reality. The living, breathing power of existence is contained within the substance of vibrations.

Every individual who is not consciously "About his Father's business" of bringing forth the vibrations of true, eternal glory by correct thinking, is wasting the powers of existence and creation.

Every individual who is not consciously and intentionally

striving to better the world in which he lives is contributing to the dark vibrations and powers of destruction. Every person who is reaching out to gather to himself wealth or power or personal glory at the expense of his fellowmen, or even of a single individual, is contributing to the delinquency of the world. And these delinquent vibrations are being amplified and hurled forth, transformed a thousandfold in magnified intensity at the present time.

Be it here known that there are many more delinquent adults and parents than there are delinquent teenagers, who are sending out their vibrations of negative darkness of uncontrolled thoughts and acts to reek havoc upon the world. The adolescent groups are receiving the greatest reactional shock because they are completely unprepared to withstand the violent vibrations that are being hurled against them by their adult elders. The young cannot cope with the magnified, intensified vibrations of evil being released into the earth's atmosphere by the thought patterns of decadent humanity. There is a prophecy which states: "And in the last days Satan shall rage in the *hearts of the children* of men."

This is a day of violence. Art is violent. Grim, hideous, even gruesome pictures are being painted of the Christ, and those who create them say they are seeking to portray all the suffering He endured, whereas they are only releasing their own dark, emotional strains, their rebellious conflicts and their evil moods as they reflect them upon His face. Even in His crucifixion no such darkened, unholy expressions ever found lodgment upon His countenance.

Entertainment is violent. Literature is violent. Modern music and dancing are no longer peaceful or graceful. They are but the eruptions of inward violence of their expressors.

Motion pictures are completely defiled with their violence. Few remaining things are beautiful in the recreational world. Television programs are also becoming overloaded with violence. And since "recreational" means to re-create, the emotions, the thoughts and feelings are being re-created into more active violence that is producing terrifying reactions by their vibrational, disintegrating powers.

Without realizing what is being done, every person who thinks a negative thought is contributing to this violence. Without knowing the cause, innocent victims, even small children, are being transformed into monsters. The world's youth is being unbalanced, blighted, outraged and destroyed, and adult delinquency is the main cause. The cure is not contained in the harsh measures of correction now being used. The cure is not in reformatories, nor in prisons, nor in capital punishment. The cause of all violence is in the adults themselves and through them the cure must come. The cause which has produced the issue must be faced and then the issues involved can be corrected and the healing come.

Child perversion, whether it be manifested through low sex impulses, disobedience, sullen rebellion, cruelty or any other negative manifestation which is being expressed in the rampant excesses, is caused primarily by children being unloved, unwanted, or punished excessively. Any child that is constantly "don'ted" is being shoved out into the negative, decadent vibrations which hold the powers of destruction. All perversions are caused by too much criticism, discord and nagging and too little love, kindly attention and trust.

Any child that is happy and loved and permitted to live

in the light will never of itself go down into the darkness, or become engulfed in the evils thereof.

"A split home" is often used as an excuse for many of the present day child problems. The split home is not as detrimental to a child as the home where the parents are filled with hates and discords. In most cases, the injury to the child was established before the actual split. The divine command of God is, "What God hath joined together let no man put asunder." This is most certainly true, but God has had little to do with most of the marriages of the present day. This is the shocking fact behind most modern marriages. It could be more rightly stated at the present time, "What man has joined together, let not even God put asunder." These reverse marriages have often been performed by supreme potentates, or the highest, most approved ecclesiastical authority and in the most exalted places on earth, yet they are not necessarily of God. Because of the hardness of heart of the children of men, the majority of marriages are simply man-made and man-performed. Without love no marriage is of God, no matter who performed it or where it was enacted.

A child has no protection built up within himself to offset the violent vibrations of parents who are not in love. No split home, with its insecurity, is as detrimental to a child as the results of continual bickering, quarreling and discordant hates and unkindness. Even hunger and want and destitution can be lived above if love is present. Nothing is as necessary to a child as love, which is more necessary to it than food or clothing. A child needs love as a flower needs sunshine. If there is no love there is usually a blighted life. And to love does not mean to spoil, to over-indulge a child. There is a great difference. Spoiled children are obnoxious to everyone. There is a happy medium, but parents need the help of the divine Father of all to find that balance.

No two children are alike. Some are more difficult, even from infancy. These are the ones who need the most love, who need to be surrounded with the prayer vibrations of the parents, rather than with over-indulgence or criticism.

The *prayer vibrations* are sent out from a loving parent's *heart*, rather than from his or her *lips*. Pray silently within your heart and send the prayer out, unknown to others. Send it on the wings of your love. And pray often. Enfolded in this vibration, any child will respond and will become a healthy, normal child.

Radical religionists have blighted as many lives as cold indifference and negation. A religion that is without love, understanding and infinite compassion is in league with the powers of darkness. Many children have been lectured and preached into hell. Many others have been driven or beaten there. None have ever gone there of their own accord.

These are the issues involved in the problems of today's abnormal, violent teenage eruptions. It has reached the point where all must comprehend the issues and face them. Adults must begin to stand up and fight the forces of evil in their own lives. Then and then only will they be able to bring a measure of balance into the lives of their children. This is a fight which cannot be carried on by sanctimonious preaching, outraged lecturing or by cowardly evasion. It must be carried out by each individual's determination to live the laws of love and forgiveness as he extends compassion out over a world staggering under the hard, cruel darkness of paralyzing negation.

To really progress it is often required for one to right wrongs he has never committed.

If you are a successful, loving parent and you think these problems do not concern you, you are mistaken. This is your world. Your neighbor's problems are yours. The world's problems are yours. If you have succeeded in keeping your own family from harm, then will you have the strength and the power to help release a world. It is such as you who are most needed, so lend your strength to redeem the earth. Let no negative thought or feeling find lodgment in your being, or go out from you.

Begin to love God as you have never before comprehended love. There are those who have desecrated, profaned and defiled the word "love" by confusing it with the fleshly sex desires. Sex is physical. It is even gross animal when uncontrolled. Love is divine, pure, unselfish and spiritual. God is love. When you think or speak of love associate it reverently with the highest impulses of your soul.

Love God with all your heart, your soul, your mind and your strength and the power of His love will be released into your hands to heal and bless and enfold a world in light.

The love of God is an actual *substance* and can be used to redeem and to glorify the earth and every human being upon it. But man must desire to be possessed by this great love in order to be able to use it. "Pray with all the energy of heart that you might be possessed of this love at the last day, that it might be well with you."

As you praise and give thanks this substance and power of His love is more readily released into your life and into your hands. It becomes more powerful and more accessible to you as you use it.

Love as you have never loved before. Drop your hates

and your bickerings and begin to pray with all the energy of your soul for the great healing to come. If you think your prayers are not necessary because you are not a parent, you err greatly. The problems are no longer just the problems of any individuals or groups or nations. These are the problems of the world as they have outgrown all private confines. They are also every individual's problems.

Pray for peace, not only to nations, but for the peace that will bring the healing into the hearts and souls of mankind. As you pray for peace for the earth and for the nations, pray for every human being in the world. Pray that the Light of Christ might begin to be comprehended and brought forth in the minds and souls of men so the great healing might come. Pray for your neighbors and your acquaintances. Whenever any individual enters your mind, surround him in love and enfold him in prayer. Do this silently and unknown to others, lest you become fanatical in the doing.

Pray that the world might be redeemed from the darkness, the violence and the unbearable evils of the present day. Pray for the youth of the world and for the adults who are blindly or indifferently causing the destruction, both to themselves and to their children. As you pray thus you will begin to help heal the great violence raging in the hearts of the children of men. You will have power to help heal the unpredictable horror destroying the youth of today who are being blighted and withered before their time of flowering, even as rose-buds in a garden can be withered and destroyed by a searing, foreign blast or an unseasonable storm.

Pray for Russia and her satellite countries. And let not your prayers arise in anguished agony, but in glorious praise and thanks for their ineffable power and the privilege you have in thus assisting the world. Pray for all nations and especially for this greatest one of all that it might fulfill its destiny as it holds aloft its banners of freedom for all to behold.

Pray, and as you pray you will take hold of the most powerful force in existence, "The love of God", to help bind up the broken, dispel the darkness and redeem a world. Through man only can the powers of God's redeeming love be used. Man is the instrument, or vehicle, through which His great love must flow forth as it carries with it the forces and powers of all healing and of all glory and all happiness. In this high vibration all darkness can be dispelled, all evils be transmuted and all mistakes transformed. Only in His love is contained the power of all good.

THE "SELF"

Chapter II.

In order to fully comprehend the good it will be necessary to further digress from the high pattern of attainment and take one last look at the evils, that they might be forever left behind. It is necessary to take this quick, penetrating look into the weaknesses of man's little mortal "self" in order to know fully the road of overcoming so that each individual might comprehend what it is he must overcome in order to complete the journey into the Light and be able to abide in that highest vibration—even heaven.

He who can become the least will be given power to become the greatest. To become the least one must give himself over completely to the will of God. In such complete surrender nothing but God's will matters to the individual. His love soars on wings of glory to embrace the very stars. He is no longer concerned with his own personal life. It no longer matters to him whether he lives or dies, endures trials and vicissitudes, or lies down in green pastures. He loses his life that he might find the greater life—of service. With his eyes wholly single to the glory of God he becomes filled with the divine vision of perfection. And henceforth he beholds only perfection, even as God holds that supreme vision always before Him.

It is by vision that all things come forth. The power of vision, or the power to imagine (image in) is the power of creation. And it is by pure, high vision that all evils can be overcome, or transformed into blessings.

It is only by deep love and praising devotion that one can blend his own life so perfectly with the mind and will of God that he becomes the expressor of the "Greatest".

This condition may sound impossible, even undesirable to those who are still lost in the cravings of the flesh and who love the little mortal "self" with its dwarfed, selfish traits, its prides and personal lusts and desires. But to him who has lifted his vision to the heights, where his eyes become single to the glory of God, it is the great achievement that fulfills all things. It is the supreme accomplishment, the sublime attainment. It is the point of power.

With this power, which one receives through the inner conquest of the "self" and the deadly "I disease", one becomes a master of himself, his surroundings and all conditions connected with his life.

It is this little mortal "self" with its sin (of separation from God) that must be comprehended. This little ego-filled "self" is the block to the way of glory and full accomplishment. It is the little mortal "self" that stirs up all discords and keeps one out of tune with the great healing, restoring, perfecting symphony of the Universe, or with the outflowing glory of the Spirit of God and Its love.

In many ancient religions and in numerous modern ones, this "self" has been understood to be "the great retarder". Various methods have been instigated and used to overcome it. The Buddha used the method of fasting and begging. The yogis of India still do. But some of the yogis are completely defeated by their own method, for as they let go of all earthly claims and possessions and become separated from the multitude they take pride in their exalted achievement. The title "holy men" becomes their stumbling block, for as they are filled with pride and satisfaction at being exalted above their fellowmen they become self-righteous. Their beggarship becomes a source of pride and though they assumed it for the sake of righteousness it becomes only the outward show of empty vainglory. It is no longer righteousness but only its ugly shadow—self-righteousness.

Anything which causes a man to take pride in the little mortal "self" is self-righteous and is empty and barren of all good. In the beginning of his endeavor, one could give all that he possessed to the poor and his body to be burned and yet, without the great Christ-like, selfless love, it would be vain and worthless. Any service to God that is lifted in pride to the exaltation of that little mortal, personal "self" is unacceptable. And so it is always this little "self" which blocks a man's way, unless it is overcome. No man is truly humble who exults in his position or his works or his own lofty seat upon the church pinnacle. No matter what his works are, as long as he is doing them to be seen of men and takes pride in the "self" or in his works, he is flaunting only the shabby, defiled garments of self-righteousness. He is only filling the seat of a Pharisee who loves his long robe and the greetings in public places and the highest seat of honor at every feast.

From the point where self-righteousness takes over all righteousness is lost. Righteousness is the ability to put God and His laws and will as the primal reality behind every act, even every thought. Self-righteousness is the continual effort to exalt the little mortal "self", to reveal its imagined importance and flaunt its mediocre works and achievements. Self-righteousness is more concerned with exalting the little personal "self" than it is with exalting and glorifying God.

It is not just among those who may consider themselves specially anointed ones that this great deception is permitted to destroy one's endeavors. It is waiting at almost every turn of the road of man's upward climb and will deceive even the very elect if they are not humble. It is humility and love which make an individual "elect". Self-righteousness and humility are incompatible. Self-righteousness and righteousness are utter strangers, enemies to each other with nothing in common. It is impossible for them to exist together. And many a proud man who thinks he is most righteous is only deceiving himself, or is permitting himself to be deceived as he serves only the forces of darkness in his unrecognized self-righteousness. Any service that is rendered without perfect love and pure humility, with eyes single to the glory of God, is rendered to the "self" instead of to God. And any individual who renders this proud self-service is no longer traveling upward, as he supposes, but downward into the darkness.

Self-righteousness is deadly in its complete destructiveness of power, and there is a little of it in almost every man. It is that "little" that can complete the downfall of those who would attain unto the heights unless it is comprehended and replaced by true humility and the pure, love-filled devotion.

Jesus said, "A certain man went down from Jerusalem to Jericho, and fell among thieves, which stripped him of his raiment, and wounded him, and departed, leaving him half dead. And by chance there came down a certain priest that way: and when he saw him, he passed by on the other side. And likewise a Levite, when he was at the place, came and looked on him and passed by on the other side." The priest was on his way to the temple to fill an important place in a very high service to God. The Levite was on his way to burn incense to the Lord. Each in his pride believed himself to be the most chosen and righteous among men and theirs was only self-righteousness and they knew it not. The greatest service to God may sometimes be rendered by relinquishing an opportunity to serve in some outward capacity, to be seen of men.

There are millions of instances in modern times that are as vain and filled with self-righteousness as were the works of the Priest and the Levite.

True righteousness is the right use and comprehension of the powers and laws of God's Kingdom. Righteousness is an inclusive understanding and a humble devotion to His divine, higher laws. God's powers can never be used except in selfless, loving devotion and deep humility.

Neither can God's power be used in arrogance, nor in domineering bigotry of flaunted authority. Nor can the powers of God ever be used for self-satisfaction, nor for the glorification of the individual using them. The laws of righteousness are most holy and infinitely pure. No impure person can hold them in his hands, for he must first be purified and cleansed from all sin. He who takes hold of the eternal powers of God and then seeks to use them to exalt himself or to demonstrate the power of his position and importance will fail—or fall. Anyone who uses the tiniest iota of God's power in pride and arrogance will find that he has laid his hand upon the razor's edge. And that razor's edge is the pruning knife of the Father. That knife will cut away all dead and lifeless twigs and branches and all inferior traits. This pruning process, as the knife is held in the hand of the "Husbandman", is painful and very humiliating. It is always the most humiliating experience possible to endure unless the individual, knowingly and with humble understanding, begins of himself to bring that strident, pompous, little mortal "self" into subjection. When an individual sets his own hand to such a task it becomes a work of glory and a magnificent achievement.

Everything that is wasted, lifeless, fruitless and barren of productivity is centered in the little ego "self", with its distorted ideas of importance and its worthless traits.

Those who will not accept God's divine pruning or submit themselves to disciplinary training will find that they can never become disciples of Light. A disciple is one who begins to discipline himself. Those who discipline themselves do not need the humiliating, painful trimming of the Father's knife. Those who begin to eliminate their own weaknesses and traits that are selfish and evil will find instead of the pruning knife the loving hand of the Father extended in solicitous understanding. To those who fail to discipline themselves, or those who rigidly set themselves against the pruning knife of the Father, "the road of Holiness" will be forever closed. At least it will be impossible for them to cross over it until in time the complete humiliation of their bigotry and failures crumbles the *little false idol of themselves* into dust. If one is willing to permit this little ego-filled "self" to be thus humbled in shame, even though he has failed to accomplish the "righteousness" through self-discipline, it will still be possible for him to be reclaimed and redeemed, though his transgressions were the usurpation of the very powers of God.

Any individual who mentally or verbally condemns or judges another is doing so in the pride of his own "self-righteousness." Only proud self-righteousness ever places itself upon the judgment seat. And the law is, that: "As a man judges, so shall he be judged." Such a one is only proving himself to be empty of love and compassion. He is revealing his own *self*-righteousness as he places himself in a category of unworthiness, becoming an accuser. Only the little mortal "self", completely deceived and lost in arrogance and self-righteousness, could or would condemn his brother. If his love is great he would not even behold his faults. The truly *righteous* man sees only through the eyes of love—and in his love his brother can be healed. It is true, "That when one's mind and lips have lost the power to hurt and wound his voice will be heard among the Gods."

Self-righteousness is only one of the phases and expressions of the ugly, little, mortal, ego-inflated "self". Now, we must view it from another angle in order to comprehend its evils in their fullness.

One of those other aspects is self-pity. Self-pity is the point one reaches in the twilight of his soul when he opens wide the gates of darkness and bids the deep night enter and submerge the light. And throughout his dark night, which sometimes never ends, he gives himself over to almost unbearable anguish as he becomes entangled in the debasing vibrations of despair which have the power to strangle all hope of joy, progress and happiness. His strength is sapped and his vision blurred as his very will to fight is drained away.

It is in such deep distress of enfolding gloom that lives become warped, souls destroyed and minds shattered. It was to such as these to whom God issued these words: "Gird up now thy loins like a man—". As one girds up his loins he is prepared to fight an honorable fight against such repulsive darkness, no matter what its cause or how great it is. And in such determination, he will be given power to triumph and to overcome. It is only when one gives up and weakly wallows in the depths of self-pity that it is possible for him to be overwhelmed by it. Any individual who will put up even the slightest battle against such evil will emerge the victor. It will flee at even a strong glance, a spoken word of command, a keen, comprehending look or the tiniest manifestation of demonstrated courage. It is a coward and always hits below the belt in its own cowardly way. Yet it will always flee before any definite resistance. Its power is contained in man's lack of understanding as he permits it to defile his life.

"For we wrestle not against flesh and blood, but against principalities, against powers, against the rulers of the darkness of this world, against spiritual wickedness in high places." (Eph. 6:12)

Self-pity is the most dangerous and destructive aspect of the "self". It is the doorway into the "Nether Regions". But be it known that no individual can be enticed or forced into its debasing realms who is not completely willing. Any individual who will put up the least struggle against such vile, repulsive, decadent evil can be the victorious conquerer of it and the darkness it represents. It is only man's great ignorance and lack of understanding that has given the darkness such power. It has been a rejection of the Christ-light, through the same ignorance, that has caused man's failure to comprehend the great issues involved.

It is not deliberate wickedness but only man's complete lack of knowledge that has left him so weak a prey to the forces of such subtle evil. It is only through ignorance that he has permitted himself to be desecrated in so unholy a degree. And it has been a rejection of that divine Light of

Christ that has caused the blind ignorance that has engulfed the world.

It is from the vile "Nether Regions" of self-pity that one views every act and condition of life in a distorted, magnified, grotesque, hideous, impossible aspect. It is in this realm that all resentments and hates are injected into the bloodstream of one's being, to penetrate the body and the mind with paralyzing, decadent corrosion, as the soul becomes enslaved and bound. Within the grasp of self-pity are contained the complete powers of each man's destruction if he will not seek to rise above its deep, searing ugliness. Self-pity warps and destroys more lives each year than all the wars and all the accidents in the whole world.

The door of self-pity is always open to every man if he chooses to recognize it, or to enter therein. In fact, one has but to approach it to feel the pull of its power. There is no one on this earth who is not tempted to enter into its deadly, evil precincts to wallow in its repulsiveness at certain moments of life. But it is only those who willingly accept its invitation who are completely deceived by its hidden, subtle, defiling powers as they fly to its embrace upon every minor occasion. These are usually the ones who finally give themselves permanently over to its destroying desolation. There are millions who have become its warped, repulsive victims. It robs men of their manhood and women of their glory. It fills the mental institutions with patients and the slums with their overloads of broken humanity.

Upon every individual who abides for any length of time in the regions of self-pity there are the reeking vibrations of repellence clinging to their very bodies. This subtle vibration begins to assume the dimension of repulsiveness to those who are not also defiled by it. "Misery likes company" for the simple reason that those who wallow in their misery are repellent to the sons and daughters of light.

Few have had the understanding to look into the foul deceptiveness of self-pity with clear vision so that they can behold its desolating powers and its craven defilement. Any individual, no matter how weak or seemingly unimportant or forsaken, who refuses to be enticed into the embrace of self-pity's abhorrence will develop strength to resist and overcome it. No individual on earth can utterly fail or be conquered by circumstances if he will only gird up his loins and fight back. It takes so little effort, when one understands, to overcome this great enemy of Light. It can most easily take hold of those who blur their vision and bind their courage by the use of alcohol. Any weak dissipation oils the skids into those "Nether Regions" of heartbreaking defilement.

Not only self-pity, but even the doorway to it can be so easily destroyed before that divine, loving song of praise and gratitude to God. In praising thanks the very doors to the "Nether Regions" can be conquered and sealed forever. Its stench never permeates or even touches the garments of him who gives glory and loving praise to God.

It is often very shocking to learn that self-pity is not only a repelling factor in one's life but that it also carries a stench with it most offensive to all sensitive people. This is the reason those in the slums are avoided by the rest of humanity. It is not because mankind is judging or even disliking them. Most individuals do not know why a trip into the slums is so depressing. Neither the victims nor the rest of the world comprehend that this aversion to those defiled by self-pity is caused by the reeking vibrations of darkness which ascend from the lowest sewer level of the dark regions through its unholy victims. The vile vibrations actually become embedded in the bodies and in the very garments of those who abide mentally on that level. These vibrations become a permanent reality in all those who permit themselves to willingly remain in their repulsive depths. None can remain there who put up any effort of resistance.

No individual who comprehended its deadly vileness could possibly be enticed into the corrosive defilement of self-pity. Only a lack of understanding has caused the magnificent race of man to become so tragically, inertly blind.

These truths are now revealed that man might become free. These truths are not revealed to judge or condemn any individual. They are written only to enlighten the world as the great love of God is at last being poured out without measure, that the great healing might come. Any individual who will only make the slightest struggle, no matter how weak and erring he has been or may be, will receive help.

Blessed humanity, lost in the darkness that has engulfed the earth through the great ignorance, I implore you to shake off the apathy of the age and join the forces of Light to help redeem a world. Know that all seeming slights, hurts, misfortunes, evils and distresses can be instantly transmuted into infinite power and glory as one turns his back upon that open door of whimpering loathsomeness, which is the retreat of the coward and the weakling. But no man is naturally a weakling or a coward. Each man is noble and divine. It is only the great ignorance that has caused man to be so tragically enslaved by the forces of darkness. Each descent into the depths by any individual has but increased the blindness and the weaknesses.

To him who refuses to be enticed into such craven depths and him who makes even the slightest struggle to resist, there is always given adequate power and strength for his needs. "To him who hath shall be given!" To him who has even the slightest desire to overcome will be given strength and courage and all the help required to arise in triumphant conquering glory.

Every dark condition of failure, distress or heartbreak can become a glorified, lighted stepping-stone into the higher realms of achievement to him who selects his road and travels it determinedly.

It never matters what happens to a man. It is only how he reacts that decides the results. It is always in man's reactions, not in his actions, that the greatest testings take place. It is his reactions to outside happenings which decide his failure or develop his strength. The deepest distresses, the greatest set-backs, the most heart-rending conditions have been used from time immemorial as a leverage to superhuman achievement by those who have become great. This is a truth that has existed in all ages and in all lands. It is always upon the ruins of failure that success is born.

The great and the noble were not necessarily endowed with a special title on success. The laws they used belong to the whole human race and to every and any individual included in it who will only fulfill the law. Success is based upon law. It belongs to him who refuses to accept defeat. The laws of happiness and achievement belong to every human being. These laws have only failed to bring the full glory of victorious rewards to those who have used them amiss, or to exalt themselves at the expense of the rest of mankind. Any individual, group or nation who seeks to exalt himself or itself through the enslavement or the sacrificing of others will be destroyed by the same laws that would have exalted him or it had the laws not been misused.

Within each difficult problem, seeming failure, desolating loss or heart-rending set-back is locked the great, stupendous power for complete, triumphant, progressive achievement.

As through love and devotion, one learns to turn to the Christ Light centered right within himself, he releases the hidden powers of his own soul. These great powers are connected with the very powers of eternity. Within this Christ Light is contained all the beautiful desires, hopes, aspirations and exquisite dreams of longed-for glory and the complete power of fulfillment. Within this holy Light nothing is lacking of all that is good and desirable, permanent and real.

It is in this Light of higher understanding and vision that one is given the ability to overcome. One learns to ride upon the storm—above it—beyond it, for it cannot touch him.

Within every condition is locked unspeakable power for good, or for ill. It is for man to say which it shall be.

It is always the little mortal "self" that stands in the way of each man's divine, spiritual progress, whether it be operating through self-righteousness, self-pity, self-importance or self-indulgence, which alone can cause him to remain on a par with the animals. Any of the attitudes that concern the pompous "self" are the traits that block one's road to happiness and glorious achievement. These little selfish, deceptive attitudes and traits of the flesh are the enslavers of the race of man. They are also the doorways into the lower regions.

It is only the little, insignificant, mortal "self" that gets its feelings hurt, its pride injured, that retaliates mentally or physically to injuries of any kind, real or imagined. It is only the little "self" that becomes strident, rebellious or filled with discordant, retaliating confusion of hates. It is only the little "self" that is ever betrayed and overwhelmed by the fleshly appetites and lusts. It is the little "self" that slinks away and refuses to face issues in which are contained all the opportunities of progress and powerful growth and fulfillment. It is the little "self" that becomes engulfed in jealousies and malicious dislikes. It is this little "self" that blocks the way to each individual's own divine, glorious destiny. It is this little mortal "self" that contains all the approaches into the realms of hell.

This little mortal "self" is each man's greatest enemy, and "He who can learn to rule it is greater than he who rules a city." This little "self" is the sin. This little "self", with its false ego, its insatiable hunger for attention, its desires to be first and most important, its endless efforts to always try to save face or protect its pride, is that within man which separates him from God. It is this little mortal "self" that has constructed *the veil of unbelief.* This little mortal "self" is the veil. This little "self", that is nurtured and developed by the five physical senses refuses to believe anything that it has been unworthy to experience, or too spiritually blind to behold. This little "self" has held entombed the Light of Christ as it has sought to exalt itself.

This little "self" is man's consciousness which has been cast out of the presence of God because of transgression, and has been left to wander in a lone and dreary world—

the world of "self". It is this little physical, mortal "self" that has left the light and warmth of the Father's house to pound itself to pieces in the realms of outer darkness.

It is this little "self" that has taken over the rulership of man's being and has caused him to abide in the great outer darkness, lonely and confused, poor, wretched, miserable and blind and naked.

Every intense personal desire which excludes the rest of mankind and is contrary to the laws of unselfish, honest, honorable living is only the loud, clamorous voice of the little mortal "self" seeking to deceive and entangle one's life in its blinded usurpation of power and empty importance.

Christ, when He healed individuals, did not always say, "Go thy way, and seest that thou tell no man." No. Only occasionally did He impart this strict injunction. This command was given only to those who were inclined to brag. There were those, even in the days of Christ, who would have gotten more satisfaction out of telling that they had been singled out for healing by the famous Galilean than in the healing itself.

More great and noble ones have been betrayed by the pride of their acquaintances who have basked in their own self-importance than through personal prejudice or a desire for "thirty pieces of silver." Public attention and acclaim have been more important to many individuals than their integrity. Pride is the great betrayer of trusts and the greater betrayer of friends. And all pride is but the little, mediocre, mortal "self" in true expression.

My own betrayals were always from those who were very near and very dear to me. None of them had any particular desire to really injure or destroy me. They only desired to establish their own importance by acclaiming things which were not always true and sometimes revealing facts which they had pledged themselves to hold as sacred. But with this inner understanding it is so easy to say, "Father, forgive them for they know not what they do."

It is when the little mortal "self" leads one into great darkness, wickedness or violence that it must be checked. Conditions have reached the point of such bigoted violence today the very world itself could be destroyed, along with all the pompous pride and prejudices created by man's swaggering, self-encouraged, mortal "self", as each fills his own little niche of exaggerated importance.

It would be hopeless indeed if behind this seeming decadent worthlessness did not lie the jewel of eternal, indestructible glory—the divine TRUTH.

KNOW THE TRUTH

Chapter III.

The more one is engrossed in the "self", in its prides, vanities, lusts and desires, the deeper he is in the darkness and the further he is from the TRUTH. And the further a man is from the TRUTH, the less light he has to guide and direct and glorify his life, consequently the greater are his errors and mistakes and weaknesses though he may actually believe he has his feet emplanted in Celestial realms and his hands upon the very throne of God. Thus his own conceit deceives him and robs him of eternal light as the powers of the Almighty are retarded in his life.

It must be here understood that every individual is either ruled by his own little, mortal, ego-filled "self" as it pounds and pushes him along into its dark, erroneous ways of floundering, deadly mistakes, or he begins to reach upward toward God in a searching humility that must fulfill the promise, "Seek me diligently, and ye shall find me", if one will only continue his seeking.

As one *even begins to BELIEVE* in that "Light of Christ that is given to abide in every man who cometh into the world", and starts the inward search to contact that divine Light, he is on his way into exalted realms. And no man can truly seek for this Light without finding It. For "He who seeks finds." And, "Unto him who knocks it shall be opened." As one searches, his faith turns into knowing and knowing turns into power. The *knowing* is that divine contact with the Light. As one continues his search he automatically becomes "Purified and cleansed from all sin." And sin is the "self". It is every thought, feeling and vibration that is out of tune with the great symphony of the universe.

It is as one progresses into the Light, continuing in his search for the Kingdom of God and the right use of its divine laws of perfection, that the little mortal "self" is outgrown and left behind. As it is overcome it will be transformed into Light. Even as all negative forces can be transmuted into power, so can the little mortal "self" be translated into "ONE" with the great, divine Light.

It is not possible to enter this divine Kingdom of Heaven, which is the kingdom of awakened understanding and infinite power, by just weakly desiring it. One must first comprehend just what issues are involved, and by his own awakened choice decide whether he will serve the darkness or advance into the Light. He must continue to use his free-agency, as he always has, if he has not already forfeited it to sin. And if it has been thus relinquished, he must begin the battle of his life to recapture this priceless possession, for he is completely impotent without it. He must use this free-agency henceforth with the knowledge of just what is involved. With his understanding opened he becomes completely and fully accountable. He also becomes endowed with the power to fulfill speedily the laws of either realm.

In man's very searching, reaching and desiring to leave the darkness the ability to *believe* is developed—and is perfected. It is when one is smugly satisfied with the darkness and with his own little meager, mortal "self" that he remains in the darkness, unenlightened, unprogressive and devoid of power.

With awakened vision each man will be able to see
clearly the road into the light as he recognizes the subtle
by-roads of "self". Each trait of "self" is recognized as an
enticing guide-post to the lower levels of life. They are
also indicators to the higher realms of exalted existence as
they are by-passed in that upward climb into the eternal
light of glory and divine achievement.

As one *believes in* and then begins to comprehend that
inner Christ Light, which holds within it all the redemptive
powers Christ came to give, he is no longer "under condemnation". The great, holy Christ-powers of redemption
enfold such a one in their exalting, purifying, forgiving,
redeeming glory.

It is impossible to attain fully unto the Christ Light without loving God with one's entire being, his heart, his soul,
his mind and strength. And "The nearer one approaches
perfection the clearer are his views, and the greater his enjoyments, till he has overcome the evils of his life and lost
every desire for sin; and like the ancients, arrives at the
point of faith where he is wrapped in the power and glory
of his Maker and is caught up to dwell with Him. But we
consider that this is a station at which no man ever arrived
in a moment; he must have been instructed in the laws and
government of that kingdom by proper degrees, until his
mind is capable in some measure of comprehending the
propriety, justice, equality and consistency of the same."

With man's growing comprehension, as he reaches upward his eyes become single to the glory of God instead
of to his own glory, and in that singleness of love and
dedication "he becomes like the thing he gazes upon"—
even the Light. He beholds Christ as one who gazes in a
mirror! And he himself begins to take on that reflection.

The very mirror is the lighted brilliance of his own soul as it becomes purified. That mirror is the gold of himself that has been tried in the fire.

This gold, or mirror of a man's own soul becomes a glorified reality as it is completely purified. This purification is accomplished as the gold is separated from the dross—or sin, which is the trait of "self". The dross has always been the little mortal "self" with its greedy lusts for pomp and show, its vain hopes and desires for the highest seats, its evils and discords and its animal appetites. This little "self" has contained all the evils of each man's life. It is the dross that has defiled the gold and made it unusable and kept it in an unglorified condition of unworthiness.

We have now reached the time the ancient prophets told about—the time when all men would be able to "discern between the righteous and the wicked".

The righteous are all those, who through their developed power to *believe,* contact that Christ Light within and begin to bring it forth in their own lives until they become filled with It, and Its power. "For My Kingdom is not in word, but in power," saith God. It is the time when all those who only profess such divine contact with the powers of God, yet preach their empty sermons of words or live their mediocre, unexalted lives devoid of His Light and His power, will be instantly recognized. Often the shame of such, with their empty hands and their vacant souls, will be greater than the shame of those who realize they are lacking and sinners. The sinners make no such false claim upon righteousness, hence there is no hypocrisy in them. But whether a man is a professed sinner or a falsely professed saint, he will be recognized for what he is. His light and his darkness will both be plainly discernible.

The wicked are all those who are still lost in the darkness of the little mortal, physical, ego-filled "self" with its prides and prejudices, its fleshly desires and intense likes and violent dislikes. Wickedness can be either a degree of rebellious defiance or its opposite, the inflated idea of self-righteousness. Both are conditions caused by the great ignorance of not comprehending or contacting that Divine Christ Light.

From the higher realms it is surprising to note that the sinner and the over-inflated minister on the exalted pinnacle of the church may be equally engulfed in the darkness of "self". In fact, the minister, or he who professes to be the most enlightened, may be even more engulfed in that darkness than the other. The weakness of hypocrisy, the inflated, deceptive works of the religious acclaimants may be as great as or even greater than the transgression of the sinners. Both are a lack of understanding of that divine, holy Light of Christ. The difference is that one professes to have all knowledge, though he has it not and is without power, while the other may inwardly realize he is only a failure, a sinner, or however else he may feel about himself.

Many who profess to hold the very keys of heaven in their hands will, in their moment of great revelation, be completely overwhelmed in an almost overpowering, crushing, devastating humiliation. If they can, in that moment of severest trial, not seek to cover their shame by self-justification, they might still have the ability to be delivered and redeemed from the tyranny of that little ego-filled "self" as they let go of all pride, all self-adulation, self-importance and instinctive self-justification, even while they are being invited down from the highest seat to take a lower one. And may God's special love enfold them in its healing mercy at that time.

Criminals have often been reclaimed in an instant when they have reached the bottom and drunk of the bitter dregs of life. Locked in solitary confinement, criminals have sometimes been given the power to behold the loving rays of Christ's enfolding light and have changed. Others have picked themselves up from some filthy gutter and walked right out of their unholy environment and its impossible evils. And there are also those who have suddenly found themselves in some vile dive with manhood, funds and life completely spent, who in an agony of engulfing remorse found their lost souls. There are thousands more of those who have been classed as sinners who are but awaiting the gentle touch of Christ's Light to submerge the little evil "self" in a complete letting go of utter surrender as the Light takes over with its healing.

"Two men went up into the temple to pray; the one a Pharisee, and the other a publican. The Pharisee stood and prayed thus with himself; 'God, I thank thee, that I am not as other men are, extortioners, unjust, adulterers, or even as this publican. I fast twice in the week, I give tithes of all I possess'.

"And the publican, standing afar off, would not lift up so much as his eyes unto heaven, but smote upon his breast, saying, 'God, be merciful to me a sinner'.

"I tell you, this man went down to his house justified rather than the other: for every one that exalteth himself shall be abased; and he that humbleth himself shall be exalted." Luke 18:10-14.

He that humbleth himself will never need to be humiliated. Only the proud, self-righteous man can or will be humiliated as he is invited down from his exalted position to take some lower seat.

Sin is only the little mortal "self" in complete expression. The "self" contains the darkness, the evils and the powers of transgression. It contains the prides and selfishness that separate a man from God. It is the separation from God that is the great sin. It is the separation from that divine Light of Christ within that holds all the powers of sin and error. And it is the acceptance of the Light of Christ that holds the power to overcome sin and the power to redeem one from its effects and influences.

It is not just the little faults and failings in a man's character, not his erroneous actions and mistakes or even his great sins which will bring his judgment. Neither will any man be condemned or judged for his weaknesses, nor by what the world has termed as "sin". Man is only condemned by his rejection of that Light of Christ that has been given to abide in him. Each individual's failures, mistakes and transgressions are in themselves only the effects of the great cause. Each man's own rejection of that divine Light of power and eternal glory has been the great cause of all sin. Sin is but the result of the engulfing darkness that takes over when that divine Light is not accepted. There is only the one great sin which is the cause of all the evils, weaknesses, mistakes and errors. This one great sin is the rejection of the Christ-Light. This rejection alone holds the power of condemnation. This rejection is the one great cause. The weaknesses, failings and all consequent evils are but the results of the one great sin, the rejection of His Light, which is given to abide in every man who comes into this world. In this great rejection the "self" has been permitted to take over and to rule in its blindness and selfishness and physical lusts. This has been the cause of man's separation from God. It has been the little mortal "self" that has not only refused to acknowledge this glorious, redeeming Light of Christ, but has determinedly fought against It. And it is His Light that holds all power and glory and fulfillment in its scope of purified exaltation.

Often those in high places are even more engulfed in this great sin than the recognized sinner. But regardless of who is involved it is only the great ignorance of His Light that has caused all sin. It is only the separation from God, in consciousness, that condemns into outer darkness. It is only the little mortal "self" that can possibly separate man from God and keep him in the great vortex of evil, for all darkness is only a lack of the Christ Light which man himself has rejected, whether he be a sinner or a professed prophet. It is only the mortal "self" that fulfills the great hypocrisy of self-righteousness as it usurps the power and authority of God in its pride and arrogance. And it is the mortal "self" which contains the ability to wallow in the realms of either hidden or open sin. The "self", in every individual, is but the complete expression of everyone who remains under condemnation for having rejected the Light of Christ. These have consequently remained unenlightened, hence unredeemed. Those who have not rejected that divine Christ Light will have It plainly manifested in their works of power. When this Light is comprehended and brought forth, "all will be able to discern between the righteous and the wicked." There can be no possible mistake. When that Light is fully brought forth even the blind will be able to behold It in those they meet—and that Light will heal their blindness, so they too will comprehend It and glorify God by bringing It forth within themselves.

All of mankind's errors and mistakes, its weaknesses and transgressions have been bred and fostered in the little mortal "self" as it has blundered through life without the Light.

All negative traits and conditions are but the results of the one great sin—the sin of Separation from God—the sin of "self" as the Light has been rejected. "But your iniquities have separated between your God, and your sins have hid his face from you." (Isa. 59:2).

As one comprehends the great truth behind weaknesses and sins he will never again judge nor condemn another for any fault, failing or transgression. He will view the cause of such conditions with divine understanding. He will realize fully it is only a lack of knowledge which has caused that erring individual to travel his lost road, alone and desolate, bereft of the Light. That one has been blind and has not known it. The one who understands will become aware of God's goodness and realize that but for His grace he too would have remained blind.

Those who are lost in the sins and weaknesses of the flesh have never even comprehended that there is such a Light given to abide right within themselves, hence they have never contacted It nor brought It forth. It is because man has refused the invitation to "ask, seek and knock" that he has remained in blindness, consequently has not been aware he was being led by those who were also blind. As one's understanding is expanded by the Light, the one great sin remains visible in all its heartbreaking simplicity, the rejection of the Christ Light as each individual has in his ignorance permitted the darkness.

With this higher vision no man could possibly criticize or condemn his brother. Instead he will realize that except for the divine mercy of God he himself would have remained blind and not been given a view of the Great Light and the issue involved. Humble and love-filled, he will reach out to enfold his still erring brother in Christ's forgiving love, for as he comprehended the Light and brought It forth the power of divine love was bestowed. And it is such love, sent out to one's erring brother, that that brother can be healed.

The most surprising TRUTH of all will be revealed fully when one begins to use the developed, glorified Light of Christ, brought forth and perfected right within himself, in this manner. It will be noted then that often a humble, broken "sinner" may be more easily reclaimed than one who has seated himself upon the lofty pinnacle of the temple to be seen of men.

As each man begins to believe in and to comprehend the great Light of Christ that has been given to abide right within himself and to bring it forth, he will be purified and cleansed from all sin. He will also "Be filled with Light and comprehend all things". And in this clear vision and purified love he will be healed. Then with his own expanding love he will help to heal his brother. Thus the great healing of mankind, and of the nations will commence and be carried to full fruition.

Every individual who accepts the Light of Christ, which is given to abide right within himself, will automatically leave the little mortal "self" behind with its weaknesses and errors and blundering, heartbreaking mistakes. This is how the redemptive powers of Christ work in a man's life. This is how one goes beyond the great condemnation and becomes one with the Light as he is enfolded in Its exalting, purifying glory of divine healing.

It is as simple and beautiful and as powerful and as eternal as that. The truths of God hold no great mystery. And a knowledge of the Great Christ Light, given to abide right within man, is the great TRUTH that will make man free. It is not impossible to KNOW THE TRUTH, that one might be free. The great TRUTH is the knowledge and contact with "The Light of Christ that has been given to abide right within oneself. . . . . . . "KNOW this TRUTH and you will be free indeed."

THE HOUSE OF YOUR ENEMIES

Chapter IV

If your heart has been broken and your sensitive soul wounded by unkind words and thoughtless, cruel remarks, or if your bleeding wounds have been caused by deliberate, vicious, false, unjust and injurious actions of those who have desired to destroy you, you can be healed.

Dear one, don't crawl into the dark to lick your wounds. Don't lie quivering in your wreathing agony. Don't cling to your suffering by prolonging the intense anguish you may be carrying in your bleeding heart. And, above all, don't let resentment corrode your mind and soul.

Of course, if you love the darkness more than you love the light, the most natural thing for you to do will be to crawl away into the darkness to nurse your injuries and your grudges and resentments. And no amount of pleading on my part will dislodge you.

But, "If thou wouldst be healed", then reach out your hand for a moment and touch the Light extended to you for your full recovery. If you will but close your mind against the hurts for an instant and let the great Light this work contains enfold you with its glorified vision and its healing love, you will know the blessing offered freely for your full, divine healing.

Let me take your hand and we will go together into the house of your enemies. It is a very simple thing to do, for there is neither time nor space to the eternal scope of the mind. This will be a spiritual visit and will be accomplished through the divine thinking processes of your own mind. If your hurts were in the misty past and your enemies have long since gone from this sphere of action the healing is still as necessary, and it is possible. It will be even more welcome because those who are not encumbered with flesh will receive your overtures more readily and with greater joy. Their very progress may have been retarded by your memories of hurts and injuries, and it is possible that only you can release them into the realms where they can be healed of their mistakes. Step into the past and pour out your forgiving love to enfold them in its healing glory.

If your enemies are still here in mortality and are abiding at the nethermost ends of the earth, or only next door to you, it is possible to enter their presence and extend your healing love. Come! I will go with you and we will kneel together, even as it is possible for us to kneel before the throne of God and sing our eternal praises to Him whenever we so desire.

Let my hand enfold yours as we humbly kneel together, and with bowed heads give this prayer:

"God, our Almighty, Loving Father, in the Name of Thy Most Holy Son, the Prince of Peace, we kneel here to ask for Thy healing love to enfold us and this house and those who dwell herein. Let the divine Christ Light be brought forth in Its great power of redemption to fill this dwelling and all who may abide here. Let their hearts be softened and their seals be removed. May they be purified by His Love. May their minds be enlightened by an understanding of His great redeeming glory as their blindness is tenderly healed. Let the full power of Christ's divine Light, which is given to abide in them, be permitted to come forth that

all seals might be dissolved and all darkness and ignorance
be banished.

"God, our Father, let this great Christ Light be made
manifest in us—and in all Thy children. Let it be brought
forth at this time to fill the hearts and minds and lives of
all, especially these for whom we kneel at this time to
pray. Let all errors be blotted out forever. Let all mistakes
be forgiven and let their healing come.

"Let Thy forgiving love enfold them, even as I desire
at this time to be enfolded in Thy great forgiving love.
Let me also be healed and filled with Thy holy light and
love, even as I ask that these, whom I have considered my
enemies, might be healed.

"Father, as we kneel here together to fulfill Thy divine
law of praying for our enemies, we thank You for this
holy, divine privilege. Let only our love for You remain,
for we love You, dear Lord, with all our hearts and souls!
Our minds are filled with this love for Thee as we send
it forth with all our strength. And, dear God, please increase our strength to send it out that it might go forth
to enfold and heal a world.

"So be it! In the Name of Thy Beloved Son, Jesus Christ—
Amen!"

"Wouldst thou be healed" of your resentments and your
hurts and wounds? If you desire to be healed, then kneel
and pray this prayer with all the energy of your heart and
in deepest humility send it forth. Or, if you desire, give
a prayer of your own wording, but with the same meaning.
This is not a prayer to be heard of men. This is a prayer
of the spirit. "And he who prayeth in spirit, prayeth according to the will of God. And it shall be given to him,
even as he asketh."

As you mentally kneel in spirit in the house of those whom you have considered your enemies to offer a prayer in your great forgiving love, Reason and I will each kneel with you, one on either side. As you continue to offer such a prayer daily until your own hearts and resentments are healed you may be sure that your brother is healed also. And very soon you will know the power of prayer and the nearness of God. In this great service you will be prepared to actually know God, and in time will receive of the "Fullness of the Father".

You too will go forth cleansed and purified and healed, for you will begin to comprehend the power of the great Christ Light and Its forgiving, redeeming, restoring, healing love.

You will then realize that, though you have believed yourself to be kneeling in the house or in the midst of your enemies, they are no longer your enemies. They are your brothers in whom the Light of Christ had not been lighted until you began praying for those who despitefully used you—even persecuted you.

As you continue in your prayers each day, until all is healed, you will begin to love those whom you considered your enemies before, even as you love your own soul. You will desire them to be so filled with the healing, revealing Light of Christ that in deepest solicitude you will enfold them forever in your own protecting love.

When you carry this forgiving, healing process to the point where you feel that your transgressors have been released from the burden of their transgressions, then you will know your own healing is complete and you will stand forth free and beautiful, clothed in Light. You will have shed completely your dismal, dark robes of the hurtful, evil, depressing garments of defilement. You will be clean. You will begin to become glorious.

Thus will the great healing come and thus will you have a part in it. First to you, dear one, it will come, then to those whom you have considered your enemies—and henceforth you will be able to help send it out to heal and bless a world. In such perfect Christ-like love you will realize that you have no enemies.

Will Rogers said, "I consider no man an enemy." And it is true that Will Rogers had none. Not one man on earth disliked him or wished him harm. There were a few, in the beginning of his picturesque career, who would have forced him into their own orthodox molds. But to Will their molds were most undesirable. Free and unhampered by other men's conformity, he fulfilled his own pattern of life. Refusing to be entrapped, he sent out only love and went upon his way.

The only real enemy any man ever has is the little mortal "self" with its touchy, super-sensitive prides and its struggles to protect itself, exalt itself, glorify itself at all costs. As one begins to love his enemies, or his brothers, as he loves himself, he will have overcome that little "self" and will stand forth magnificently free—free from the shackles of earth. It is a big step, I warrant you. But the great results achieved in making such a step are far greater than the effort required to make it. It is a step into a New Day—a higher dimension of living and feeling and thinking—and be-ing.

Glory be to God for the keys of fulfillment and for opportunities so divine. Glory and praise and thanks be to Him for His nearness, for He is always just as near as you permit Him to be.

Always, as one humbles and subdues himself to kneel thus in the house of his enemies, as he prays with all the energy of heart for those who, in their tragic ignorance, sought to injure him, the very heavens open and angels from the very throne of God are sent to lend their strength. And that prayer is multiplied by many. The hosts of heaven join in to send it forth, a singing melody. It encompasses the world, then wings its way across the universe. A prayer so great goes forth clothed in living flames of glory to find its way to the very highest heaven, even to the throne of God.

Prayers are always answered. And according to the unselfish intent of the pray-er are they glorified. The pray-er will, in time, be clothed in the very glory of his own exalted prayers. He will become the very glory his prayers express as he sends them forth from his own forgiving heart, opened and filled with love.

The most comforting knowledge connected with the privilege of prayer is that one need never make an appointment to enter the Presence of God and kneel thus in humble love and melting adoration. Nor need one feel unwelcome or unwanted or even rushed as he lingers to talk with God, even as one man talks with another. There is no rush, for time is not. He can linger to tell even the smallest details of his problems, if he so desires. And then, if he remains very quiet, he will learn to hear God's answers.

At first those answers may be only the silent promise of peace as it enters his heart. This is the "Holy Spirit of Promise" bearing witness to one's soul that all will be well. This is the assurance that the prayer has been heard and will be granted in His own time, in His own way and that henceforth the individual can leave it in the hands of the Father. This is the point where one learns to believe that those things, which he saith when he prays, will be given, and he shall have whatsoever he saith." This is the point of contact with that divine Light of Christ as it begins to become operative in the life of the individual.

"Therefore I say unto you, all things, whatsoever you ask when ye pray, believe that you shall receive them; and they shall come unto you. And when you shall kneel to pray forgive, if you have aught against any man; that your Father also, who is in heaven, may forgive you your sins." (Mark 11:24-25, Latin Vulgate). This is the law of fulfillment. And this is the point where one learns to believe in his own prayers, and in the power of God to fulfill them. It is not up to the individual to work out the answers. All that is required of him is to give thanks constantly that it is being taken care of. God has never failed to fulfill His own divine promises or assurances, nor to back up His Word.

Learn to enter into this divine power of consultation with Him and watch yourself grow into a new being, more confident, more love-filled, more abundantly happy and more abundantly free.

Prayer is the greatest power that has ever been placed in the hands of man. Few use it with understanding. Few use it at all. Some only use it in great emergencies. Some use it as a thoughtless, lifeless, empty ritual, and such praying is vain. But no individual can pray with real intent without being heard and he who is heard will receive an answer. Thus one grows into the spirit and power of prayer and begins to walk with God.

In thus entering into the Presence of the Greatest of all, The Divine Ruler of the Universe, The Great Creator, The Father of all, the Lord God of Hosts, you may be sure that you will never be belittled because you are an obscure person or poorly clad, ragged and unknown. Neither will you be rejected though you are at the very bottom of all human existence, wretched and forsaken by every physical, earthly, human hope or possibility of help. In His love are the answers to all your problems, the supply for all your needs, the power of your complete glorification and the love for your everlasting healing. Always there is His perfect desire to bestow His abundance of all good upon you.

No matter who you are or what your lack or failings, you will never be contemptuously received. God is not mocked, *neither has He ever mocked any child of His.*

The key to His Throne is humility. And the more often one approaches that Throne in prayer, the more readily he will be received. Any life that becomes a prayer will become powerful. Those who linger thus in His Presence will begin to take on the Light of His glory.

You too are His child and He loves you.

You need never even leave His Presence, if so be you desire to remain. His loving invitation is always held out to you. It is, "Come!" Seek Him with all your heart and you will find Him. Know surely that no problem can remain unanswered if it is turned over to Him. He has all answers. He has all power. And He is all love.

The only bars upon the doors that lead into His Presence are the hardened seals that man has placed upon his own heart and the seal of blindness he has placed upon his mind. Let your heart melt in tears! Let your love go out as it seeks "to know God" and you will find Him. As you melt the seals in your own heart and in your own mind, with infinite love you will help to melt them also for the whole world. Let your seals be melted! Let your love and prayers ascend! Let your heart be at peace and know that henceforth you do not walk alone.

As you begin to live the higher laws, to pray for your enemies and for those who have despitefully used you and persecuted you, you will begin to take on the very perfection of your Father.

"Love your enemies; pray for them which spitefully use you and persecute you; that ye may be the children of your Father which is in heaven—Be ye therefore perfect, even as your Father which is in heaven is perfect."

These are not just words. These are the very realities of the Higher Kingdom which, if you seek them, will add all things unto you.

"Be ye doers of the word, and not hearers only, deceiving your own selves." (James 1:22)

WALK WITH GOD

Chapter V

"Walk with me" has been the invitation to all the noble and great ones since time began.

If an ordinary individual were told that if he or she prepared himself or herself diligently there would be a welcoming invitation extended to enter the presence of the kings and rulers of the earth, such would accept that invitation with great gladness. No amount of effort would daunt such an individual or keep him from fulfilling all the necessary requirements.

Yet few are willing to make the least preparation to enter the Presence of the Divine Ruler of the Universe, the Great Creator of all. And to God, no individual is just "ordinary". To God every soul is a child fashioned from the very substance of His own divine Being, created with infinite love and designed to fulfill a great and noble destiny.

God's holy invitations, reaching across the ages, have been to all and have stood for always. They are but awaiting man's acceptance of them.

"Come unto me, all ye who labor and are heavy laden, and I will give you rest."

"How often would I have gathered you, even as a hen gathers her chickens under her wings; and ye would not."

"Seek me early and ye shall find me." Or, if you have failed to seek Him early, this invitation remains, "Seek me diligently, and ye shall find me," . . . . . "For *all* who seek find." . . . . . "Turn unto me and I will turn unto you!"

Most who have professed making such a search have failed to find God because they have sought only to find some church that would appease their inner hunger to actually *know* Him. In such substitution they have been given a dried crust instead of the divine manna, the bread of life and have not realized the bleak deficiency of those lifeless crumbs.

"This is Life Eternal, to KNOW Thee, the only true and living God, and Jesus Christ whom you have sent."

Do you *know* God? Or do you only *know ABOUT Him?* Do you *know* Jesus Christ? Or do you only *believe* that He is the Son of God who gave His life for the sins of the world?

To *know* God is something quite different than just knowing *about* Him. Thus to place one's loyalty in some church, no matter how great the devotion and sincerity, no matter how much truth that church contains, is not *knowing* God. Adherence to some church may not be an adherence to God at all.

Only by seeking diligently to KNOW God can the great promises be fulfilled. God alone must be reverenced, adored and given one's humble allegiance. If you can seek Him best through some church, if you can render your complete devotion to him through certain creeds, then do so. But never let it be the church you worship, nor its prestige you pay homage to. Never permit any man or religion to come between God and you.

"Seek *Him* diligently and you will find *Him*." Never be satisfied with anything less than the complete fulfilling of this promise.

Now, let us consider the divine invitation, "Walk with me!"

Have you ever tried to walk with Him? To walk with Him requires only that you get in step with the love and rhythm of the Universe. It is becoming in tune with all that is pure and beautiful and glorious. It is but lifting your vision to the height of His glory as the negatives and darkness are left behind. As your eyes become single to His glory, you will have to begin to take on that glory as you become filled with Light and comprehend all things. This is how one can actually KNOW God. This is how one begins to walk with Him.

Christ said, "No man can come to me, except the Father which hath sent me, draw him: and I will raise him up at the last day." (John 6:44). This last day means the last day of his testing, hence the last day of his seeking as he is lifted up in consciousness to abide in the higher realms of Light. This end is the end of his purification. It does not mean the last day of earth, as many have supposed. The whole experience is an individual thing. It is not a point in time. And it is the Father who leads one to comprehend the Christ—it is the Father who gives one the power to comprehend that "Light of Christ which has been given to abide in every man who has ever come into the world." When one comprehends that Light it is no longer a rejected factor in his life and he will no longer be under condemnation.

After the Father has drawn one to the Son, then that divine Light of Christ will reveal the Father. For, "All things are delivered to me of my Father; and no man knoweth who the Son is, but the Father; and who the Father

is, but the Son, and he to whom the Son will reveal him."
(Luke 10:22; also Matt. 11:27).

From the foregoing it must be understood that the love
and power of Almighty God, the Father, will draw one to
the Christ. Only this great love can possibly lead one to
comprehend the fullness and glory of Christ and His divine
Light. And this is the only possible way any man can
actually "Know God, and Jesus Christ, whom he has sent."
It is the only way any individual can learn to walk with Him.

"The Light of Christ, that has been given to abide in
every man who cometh into the world" has been the rejected factor, or the Chief Corner Stone that was rejected
by the builders. It has been rejected by each man as he has
constructed his earthly tabernacle, his physical body from
the elements of the earth. It is this divine Corner Stone
alone that can fulfill a man's own perfect destiny of eternal
glory. The acceptance or establishment of that Chief Corner
Stone contains the powers of all fulfillment and all glory.
In it is the power of redemption and overcoming.

"To him that overcometh will I give to eat of the hidden
manna, and I will give him a white stone, and in the stone
a new name written, which no man knoweth saving he
that receiveth it." This white stone to be bestowed is the
Christ Stone, or "The Chief Corner Stone that the builders
rejected." It is the white, translucent stone through which
the Christ Light shines forth in its pure power of glorious
fulfillment.

Only through this divine, inner Light of Christ, which has
been rejected by the builders, can one possibly *know* God
the Father, or have Him revealed. And only through this
inner striving to bring forth or contact the Light can one
ever hope to *know* Jesus Christ, Who is its source. Only

through divine contact with this inner Christ Light can one KNOW His great, unspeakable Name, the Word of all-power.

"Ask and ye shall receive; seek and ye shall find; knock and it shall be opened unto you." This is a special admonition to every individual, and each human being must fulfill it for himself. Every person, of and for himself, must make that divine search. Each must utter his own requests, send forth his own petitions and do his own knocking upon that inner door in order to be admitted into the true sanctuary of the Lord.

This intense, individual searching is not possible for those who are satisfied to let someone else lead them, find their answers and do their thinking—even their *knowing*. *Knowing* is an individual experience and condition. No man can possibly KNOW God for another. If you wish to KNOW, then *you* must cease to let the blind lead you. You must overcome that same blindness in your own mind. You must begin to remove the blindness of mind by permitting the Light of Christ to come forth, which alone can dissolve that blindness. You must awake and begin to do your own searching, your own asking and your own knocking, for *everyone* who asks receives.

If *you* would comprehend "The Secret Place of the Most High", it will have to be through your own mind that divine information is received. Or, if you yearn to enter the great sanctuary of the Lord and kneel in the Holy of Holies before that Altar of the Almighty, then learn to enter into the center of your own soul, through love and gratitude, adoring praise and deep humility, as you worship Him with all your heart, soul, mind and strength. Only in this manner can one be prepared to *know* Him, or the great TRUTH that will set him free! Only in this way is it possible to *know* God, the Father and Jesus Christ, whom He has sent.

"He that dwelleth in the secret place of the most High shall abide under the shadow of the Almighty." (Ps. 91:1).

"Hide me under the shadow of thy wing." (Ps. 17:8).

"Because thou hast been my help, therefore in the shadow of thy wings will I rejoice!" (Ps. 13:7).

As one learns to abide in the Secret Place of the Most High by learning to hold his mortal consciousness upon that ever expanding, inner Light as It is released from within himself, he will be prepared to *know* God. In this secret place, or Holy of Holies, there is no evil, for no evil can possibly exist there. It is the place of complete protection against all darkness, all evil and error. These negative aspects are completely overcome by and in this divine Light of glory. It is the place of complete and full enlightenment, where one is so filled with Light he comprehends all things. It contains all the powers of divine healing. Just to comprehend it is the complete establishment of that Chief Corner Stone and it is no longer a rejected factor in one's life. When that Corner Stone is established the Light of Christ is released and It becomes the greatest accepted factor and reality of existence. It is the power.

When this inner, Christ Light is no longer rejected, when It is reverenced and brought forth from Its entombment, then it is not only possible to *know* God and Jesus Christ, Whom He hath sent; it is also possible to "walk with Him".

To walk with God is a glory far beyond anything man has ever realized. If you have yearned for wealth that you might dwell in fine mansions, beautiful resorts, or luxurious hotels; or that you might array yourself in expensive, exquisite apparel and bedeck yourself in jewels; or ride upon the clouds as you go forth to view the wonders of the world, then your desires have been only mediocre, childish whims and empty wishes of valueless import.

As one learns to walk with God he abides in the Holy of Holies, the Secret Place of the Most High, the sacred, glorified precincts of the Sanctuary of the Lord. No mansion or dwelling upon earth can compare with the grandeur of this abode of infinite power and peace. As one walks with God he will be literally clothed in Light, in the divine White Raiment of eternal glory. And I assure you that no apparel in all existence could be more exquisitely beautiful than this. I would fain describe it if that were possible. It isn't. There are no words to reveal its divine, shimmering glory of pure spiritual beauty and breath-taking loveliness. Nor will such a one need to take some physical, mechanical vehicle of transportation to travel forth to view the wonders of the world. With his hand in the hand of God he will view the very wonders of eternity!

Yea, "Abide in me!" . . . . . "Walk with Me!" These are His invitations reaching across the boundless stretches of time, as they span eternity to find an echoing response in your own open, vibrant heart as all things are fulfilled in you.

"Walk with God" and you shall walk in majesty. As you walk thus clothed in Light, love will flow from your garments and in the majestic, everlasting power of the Almighty, you too shall be divine.

THE POWERS OF THE RESURRECTION

Chapter VI

The book, *The Temple of God,* explains much about "The Light of Christ, which is given to abide in every man who cometh into the world." It may even seem that the subject has been over-stressed in this work. If it seems so to you, I ask that you be patient, for this is the most important subject in existence at the present time. It is impossible to speak of this Light too much, or too often. This is the day of Its release. This Light must begin to be comprehended, for it is—"time".

So, if it seems that certain points are carried to a tiring degree of repetition in this work, please indulge your loving patience. There are those who are gifted in music and after hearing a melody or even a whole symphony only once are thereafter quite familiar with it. There are others who are not thus gifted. For them a piece of music must be played many times before it becomes so established within themselves they can recall a small portion of it in either a whistled or hummed refrain. Remember that no great symphony becomes less loved by repetition. Every repeated, soft refrain is like the delicate, loving handclasp of a beloved friend. So let this be to you as you open your soul to receive its every vibrant, tender tone. I promise you that back of every mellowed repetition new truth shall stand revealed.

The scriptures tell us that those who reject this Light are

under condemnation. In other words, those who reject the Light of Christ that has been given to abide right within themselves are still unredeemed. It is the Christ Light alone that holds the keys and powers of the great redemption.

This Light of Christ also contains the keys and powers of the resurrection. Christ proclaimed to the world nearly two thousand years ago, "I am the resurrection and the life; he who believeth on me shall never die."

It is true that the seed of this Christ Light has been given to abide in every man. But man, who has not comprehended the Light, has not accepted It, though millions believe with their unawakened vision that they have fully accepted all that Christ came to give. Their very lack of power betrays them and reveals their empty hands. Most religious organizations are only institutions for the blind, and they realize it not. The more fanatical a religion is and the more sure its adherents are that they hold a monopoly upon all truth, the greater is their degree of blindness.

In order for any group or individual to even begin to comprehend the great Christ Light, it or he must first *believe* that this Light does exist. One must believe it, if for no other reason than that God said it is given to abide in every man who cometh into the world. Then if he will check back over his life very carefully, he will be able to recall moments of inspiration, of unaccountable hunches or divine experiences that will assist that tiny spark of belief to grow until it becomes a living flame of complete knowledge.

Through loving praise and gratitude that inward Light may be contacted and comprehended. The speed and fullness of this comprehension will depend in a degree on the spiritual advancement of the individual. As that Light is contacted and *felt* right within, It will grow according to the love and attention one focuses upon It. Love It even as you would nurture and love a little child within you, awaiting full manifestation and expression. The more one becomes aware of that divine Light the more speedily It will be brought forth, until all the promises Christ ever gave will begin to be fulfilled. It is then one *knows* that "The Kingdom of Heaven *is* within." He also learns that "The Kingdom of God is *not in words, but in power.*"

As one begins to contact that divine Light of Christ within his own soul, he will realize that he has been the tomb or sepulcher in which It has been buried. His own hardened heart has been the stone which has sealed that Light of Christ in the tomb of his own being so It has remained a rejected factor in his life. He will realize, very repentantly, that every strident act of his own little mortal "self" has crucified that Christ Light afresh.

As that Christ Light is reverenced, accepted and brought forth, one partakes of the very powers and reality of Christ's divine resurrection—and he need never die.

This very Christ Light, when brought forth until It fills every cell and fiber of man, is the gift of life itself. "Christ is the Life" and His Light is the life of every individual. In accepting this Light of Christ within, one is but accepting the powers of Christ and the way of redemption which He so graciously offered to the world. This divine Christ Light contains all the powers that Christ came to earth to reveal and to share. It contains the powers of renewal and of resurrection. It releases the old, dead things in one's life. The worn-out cells and tissues either drop away or are quickened into new life. They are resurrected into a new phase of Spiritual existence in which "they need never die".

"Therefore it is given to abide in you: the record of heaven; the Comforter; the peaceable things of immortal glory; the truth of all things; that which quickeneth all things, which maketh alive all things; that which knoweth all things, and hath all power, according to wisdom, mercy, truth, justice and judgment."

These are the holy powers that are contained within that divine Light of Christ, which has remained but a rejected factor in man's life. The power "to quicken and to make alive" is the power of the resurrection, or the power of renewal of all the cells of the body—and the mind. According to the great loving wisdom and the mercy, truth, justice and judgment of our Almighty Father was this Light of Christ, which contains all the great gifts given to abide right within man. No individual ever came into this world who was not endowed with this great Christ Light or the gift of these supreme, almost incomprehensible powers. All the divine powers of God are still sleeping in the seed of that divine Christ Light which is still buried and rejected in the center of the soul of man. It is true that "All that the Father has is yours."

Man has remained condemned or unredeemed from his mortal failings, weaknesses, sins, errors and death simply because he has rejected the great Christ Light. Within that Christ Light is contained all the gifts, blessings and powers ever promised to man. All the gifts and promises ever given can be man's to use whenever he accepts the great Light of Christ in which they are contained.

Among the divine gifts contained in the Light of Christ is the gift of peace. This gift the Father gave freely to the world at the birth of His Beloved Son, Jesus Christ. It was a gift that belonged completely and fully to any who ac-

cepted His Son, the Prince of Peace. Yet Christian nation
has fought Christian nation from the beginning; Christian
churches have fought Christian churches; Christian men
have fought Christian men in their individual struggles to
reach the top. The world has cried, "Peace; Peace! But
there is no peace!"

The very gift of peace is contained within the great Christ
Light and as long as it is a rejected factor in the lives of
men there can be no peace, either in the hearts of men or
among the nations.

None can bring forth that divine, glorious Light of
Christ without receiving the "Peace that passeth understanding!" This peace is far beyond thought. It is a gift
of the soul and becomes the divine reality of all who possess
it. It is this great gift of peace which gives one the power
to walk in majesty, though his cross awaits. It is the majesty
that gives one the power to "Walk with God," and to
actually *know* Him. Within the Light of Christ is contained the great peace and the powers thereof. Within the
great divine Light is contained all the gifts and powers of
God, even the power to *know* God. Those who have accepted this Light and brought it forth in their lives will be
walking in the power of it and their hands will be filled
with the ineffable powers He promised.

Sin and darkness, no matter what forms or guises they
have taken, whether it has been the road of sin or the road
of self-righteous bigotry, are exactly the same. They have
both been caused by the rejection of the Light of Christ,
which has been given to abide in every man who has ever
come into this world. Only the rejection of this Light has
caused the bigotry of creeds and the crimes of the individuals.

The divine Christ Light is contacted and brought forth

most readily through the fulfilling of the greatest of all commandments.

When love pours through the great, living heart-center of one's being, the Light of Christ is released in vibrant glory as it flows through that inner center of being with its vibrating gift of eternal life.

When one loves with his whole soul, that Light is carried from the inner life-center to the life-center of every cell of the physical body and the quickening process begins in the mortal body of man. In this releasing or developing gift of love the great Light is brought forth. And this Light is the "Life eternal" promised to all those who believe.

When one loves with all his mind, its seal of blindness is removed and the power to comprehend all things is given. "For he who is filled with Light shall comprehend all things"—"even God." He will comprehend the things that have heretofore been incomprehensible, even the things of the spirit, which contains the great eternal realities of all that exists. With the coming forth of the Light the darkness and the heartbreaking sins with their inherent evils are overcome. The fears and all negation are cast out. The joys and glories of God are increased in a new and throbbing vibration of eternal life. One's life literally takes on a new and higher rate of vibration from the very moment he opens his mind to *believe* and begins his search to find. And he who takes on that vibration of Light becomes vibrant.

Go among the inert crowds of humanity who are not falsely stimulated to stages of excitement and notice the deadness, the vibrationless, expressionless decay clinging to them as they walk along with death. They may be good and mean well, but unless they begin to exert their strength in sending out love, they are not vibrant. They are living in a half-dead unawareness of the glory and powers vested right within themselves. These are the ones of whom Christ said, "Let the dead bury their dead." They are walking with death. Death is manifested in their dying bodies, their uninspired thoughts, their lack of singing glory and in the darkness of their uninteresting lives.

If you should mingle in crowds for hours upon hours looking for that singing vibrancy of joy, you would probably encounter in a whole day one or two who seemed to have that something which made others turn and look in pleased admiration.

Spontaneous youth carries more of it than its elders, because youth has not yet begun to walk with the hand of death upon it. Youth is the expression of life. And when youth carries love with it its glow is felt by everyone.

"All the world loves a lover!" Those in love are living in that higher vibration of light. They are carrying it with them and all the world loves to contact those thus embued with the invigorating fragrance of its breath. Such love, when it is legitimate, was never meant to die. Those who can hold to it throughout their lives are in a small measure walking in a more beautiful world. It would be easy for such to go another step and enfold the world in their love—and reaching on to God, receive the divine fulfillment of all power and all glory. These great earth loves are but God's gateway into the eternal powers of heaven, contained within the greater love.

Those who are without love of any kind are carrying around their ugly, black shroud of death with them. They are clothed in it. Go into bus stations, into depots and places where people are lingering and behold the hand of death resting upon their shoulders. Then tingle at that one in a hundred, or the one in a thousand who carries wings upon her feet, a song in her heart, a light in her eyes and who expresses unknowingly the vibration of life. Then search into your own soul and ask, "What is it this person has that the others lack?" If you ask them they probably could not tell you. They may not even know. But you may be sure they are living closer to that Light than are the others. They may not be aware of what, how or why. If only they understood fully they could step across with ease into the new and higher vibration of eternal life.

No person can begin to love with all his heart, soul, mind and strength without being lifted into a higher vibration. He could no more help becoming alive and vibrant than a flower could withhold its radiant color and its perfumed essence. Within the gift of love is contained the great divine Light of Christ—the gift of life eternal. And as the Light of Christ is released so are the powers of the resurrection.

We are entering the day when all tears and sorrows will end, and these things can only be ended through the acceptance of the divine Christ Light. This is the day when all will soon be able to "discern between the righteous and the wicked" or those who have developed that Light and those who have not. It is the day in which "all men will be left without excuse." Before this day there has always been the excuse of not knowing. This excuse is being dissolved and crumbled into nothingness as the great Light of Christ is being released from its tomb, right within each man.

"For ye are bought with a price; therefore glorify God in your body, and in your spirit." (I Cor. 6:20).

The power to *believe* is transformed into *knowledge* when

the Christ Light has been permitted to melt the seal upon the mind so its blindness can be healed. The first ray of this released Light produces the gift of inner vision as one's mind becomes opened. And with the increase of that Light *belief* turns into *knowing*.

Those who cannot believe anything except what their physical senses have been able to reveal to them are both mentally and spiritually blind. This blindness is more real and much more tragic than any physical blindness. The Christ Light heals all such blindness when It becomes the greatest, most glorious reality in each man's life as he comprehends and brings It forth.

All things in existence are measured by vibration in the higher realms. Vibrations are the throbbing pulse-beat of life itself. Everything is manifest through vibration. This is also true upon the physical plane but few are yet aware of it. Odors are only vibrations of released energy being registered through the sense of smell. Whether the odor be of exquisite, perfumed fragrance or the released energy of decaying substance it is but vibrations of energy reaching the nostrils. The gift of sight is the power to receive vibrations of objects as they are conveyed on waves of light energy through the eyes to the mind. Hearing is the ability to receive the vibrations of physical movements and actions as they are registered upon the ears. The five senses are the physical equipment to receive knowledge through vibration. In the higher realm vibration is comprehended as the great reality for it is energy in motion, the very force of life.

All things are measured by vibration in the higher realms. Each person carries the complete revelation of what he is right within himself. All that he was, is or desires to be is registered in color vibrations that are plainly manifest and inescapable. Nothing can be hidden. These vibrations of color also have overtones of harmony—or discord. Every shade has its own expression of odor. No lily of the field could be a hundredth part as gloriously beautiful, fragrant and exquisitely harmonized as a soul that has overcome. Each individual, arrayed in light or enfolded in darkness according to the life pattern he has accepted and lived by, is clothed in the vibrating colors of his own thought actions and emotions.

Those who accept the Christ Light are literally clothed in Light. As that Light becomes manifest the darkness drops away, leaving no stain or memory of the past errors and mistakes. They are blotted out, forgotten and forgiven in Christ's redeeming light.

In this day nothing seems to enter men's minds but the ideas of conquest—the conquest of other worlds or of this one. How little men know of God and His powers when they harbor in their minds such evils! God still rules in the lives of the children of men and when they harbor nothing but thoughts of outside conquests they are only taking the sword which will have the power to slay them. God also rules in the Universe and His dominion is in love. So be it known that no beings can go from one planet to another except in the vibrations of love and good will. Only to such is the power of interplanetary travel possible.

If men of this earth, in their unredeemed condition, were permitted to visit a few of the other planets with their mortal vibrations of lust, conquest, greed and hate, they would carry only a searing flame of destruction with them. The very vegetation would be consumed by their presence and the discordant vibrations issuing from them. The gar-

dens of glory would become lone and dreary worlds of
seared desolation. So was our own Paradise lost, our Edenic
Estate mismanaged and so has it remained unattainable.
This is still an unredeemed world though Christ came and
gave His life for its salvation. Man has not yet accepted
His gifts.

Only by the acceptance and development of the Divine
Christ Light can the earth—and man—be salvaged and redeemed. When that Light is no longer a rejected factor
and his divine gift is accepted by mankind, this whole world
will be lifted into a higher category of existence. As it stands
today, it is the lowest of the spheres and the least desirable.
The inhabitants of other worlds would not even want it.
There are worlds advanced so far beyond our sin-drenched
little earth that it and every human being upon it would
be instantly consumed by the very glory if such planets were
to approach too near.

Man has waited impotently for God to reach down and
force salvation upon him. Man has gone down that oiled
slide of sin, selfishness, darkness and error in an almost
unresisting fashion, deceiving himself in his vain and foolish
reasoning as he has convinced himself there was nothing
for him to do. He has made himself believe that Christ did
everything for him, though Christ so plainly taught that any
man who followed Him would have the power and would
be required to do the works which He did. It has been so
much easier for man to believe that none of the responsibility is his, that Christ did it all, than for him to throw
off his shackles of inertia, lethargy and sin.

As man awakes and takes hold of that Christ Light
which has been given to abide right within himself, he will
hold the very powers of heaven in his hands—and the powers

not only of redemption but of the resurrection. First he will be redeemed from every weak, false, erroneous idea, then from his sins and weaknesses, evils and mistakes, then from his bodily ailments, until his whole being is resurrected into a newness of glorified vibrant life.

No individual upon this earth need remain ill or crippled or helpless or bound in any way by physical handicaps. Neither need he lie helpless and impotent as he waits in languor for some outside person to come and heal him. All the powers of healing are contained right within each individual. Within his own being is the Light of Christ which contains all healing and all power. One has only to have faith in it to have it become more and more manifest in his life, until the great, full healing of eternal renewal can be carried to the point of a complete resurrection. There is no mystery about it. Only those who are abiding in darkness and who are without His Light seek to shroud truth in mystery. Any who whisper in awed tones of mystery are but cloaking their own ignorance and lack of light and understanding behind their own veil of darkness.

The divine Christ Light has many functions and purposes. It is the Spirit of pure intelligence. It knows all things; it comprehends all things; It has all power, and its first function is to reveal truth. Few permit it to function even in this lesser capacity. When any new information is propounded, that information is usually rejected because it was not previously included in one's stagnant, orthodox beliefs. With minds thus sealed, Christ's Light is rejected. The Light of Christ, when focused upon any information, instantly reveals the truth or fallacy of the subject. This discerning process is accomplished by taking the information into that "holy of holies", the very center of one's own soul, and placing it upon that altar of glory to permit those divine Christ rays to touch it. In those rays the subject will be completely revealed. This is the method by which one can comprehend all things.

Because proud man "trusts only in the arm of flesh", or in his own vain opinions, his unglorified, mortal thinking processes or preconceived, orthodox beliefs contained in the blindness of his own mortal mind, truth and the Light of Christ have remained rejected factors in the lives of the children of men.

Only by a conscious contact with that all-knowing, glorified, inner Light of Christ can any man judge fully between truth and error, Light and darkness.

"For behold, my brethren, it is given unto you to judge, that ye may know good from evil, and the way to judge is as plain, *that ye may know with a perfect knowledge, as the daylight is from the dark night.*

"For behold, the Spirit of Christ is given to every man, that he may know good from evil; wherefore, I show unto you the way to judge; for everything which inviteth to do good, and to persuade to believe in Christ, is sent forth by the power and gift of Christ; wherefore ye may know with a perfect knowledge it is of God.

"But whatsoever thing persuadeth men to do evil, and believe not in Christ, and deny him, and serve not God, then ye may know with a perfect knowledge it is of the devil; for after this manner doth the devil work, for he persuadeth no man to do good, no, not one; neither do his angels; neither do they who subject themselves unto him.

"And now, my brethren, seeing that ye know that Light by which ye may judge, which light is the Light of Christ, see that ye judge not wrongfully, for with the same judgment which ye judge ye shall also be judged.

"Wherefore, I beseech of you, brethren, that ye should *search diligently in the Light of Christ* that ye may know good from evil; and if ye will lay hold upon every good thing, *and condemn it not,* ye certainly will be a child of Christ."

Or, as Paul admonished: "Prove all things, and hold fast to that which is good."

Any individual can judge between truth and error if he will but turn to this divine Christ Light, that is given to abide within. This Light is an unfailing guide to all truth and all righteousness.

It is through this Light of Christ that one must begin his search "For the Kingdom of Heaven, and its righteousness." This Light will as surely lead one into all truth, to the fullness of the Christ Light, as the sun will shed forth its light when unobscured by the clouds or the darkness of night. With man, it is the darkness of his own blind, sealed mind and the cloudiness of his personal opinions that retard the Light.

As this Christ Light is used to judge between Truth and error . . . . . and It never fails in that capacity, if permitted to function . . . . . , It will be brought forth in Its fullness more speedily and perfectly. To reveal truth is Its first requisite and the irrevocable law of Its nature. It cannot fail, or leave Truth unrevealed. Man has only to open his heart and soul in adoring humility and deep gratitude as he prays for Its divine enlightenment. He has to be humble enough to put all his preconceived opinions and ideas in abeyance as he turns prayerfully and in complete trust to that Light of all-knowing power. This glorified road has been difficult for the proud little mortal "self". But it becomes the eternal glory of him who learns of Its power.

In this same manner that Light can be turned upon any problem of life. Every difficult condition, every heart-breaking situation can be straightened out and healed by the Light of Christ's power.

And so it is that one's very being begins to take on the properties of that Light until he can be "filled with Light and comprehends all things."

This is the "Great TRUTH that will make man free— and he who is free shall be free indeed!" He will be freed from his bigotry, his empty pride and prejudices, his errors and mistakes, his sins and weaknesses, his disintegrating thoughts of hates and envies and his decaying illnesses. This is the great Christ gift of redemption to every man who will accept It. It is the power of eternal life and the power of resurrection. It is the power by which all the earth and every human being can be salvaged and redeemed.

As the Light of Christ is released, one is "born of the Spirit" and he becomes spiritualized. The shackles of earth are released, mortality takes on immortality—and one need never die.

THE CANDLE IN YOUR SOUL

Chapter VII

"The weak things of the world shall come forth and break down the mighty and strong ones, that man should not counsel his fellow man, neither trust in the arm of flesh—

"But that *every* man might speak in the name of God the Lord, even the Savior of the world.

"That faith might also increase on the earth;—"

This great glory that shall fill the hearts and souls of men so all will speak with the very power of the Almighty and with a *true* knowledge that is not just borrowed, with a knowing that reaches far beyond *belief,* will be, whenever mankind comprehends that Light of Christ that has been given to abide in every individual in this world. It will be when that Light has been accepted, fully comprehended by each individual and then brought forth into the fullness of divine knowing. It will be then that each and every man's life will become a thing of glory. It will be then that this world will be redeemed. For then, "A knowledge of the Lord will cover the earth even as the waters cover the sea."

It will be quite different from this day in which hundreds and even thousands of preachers proclaim that which they have never experienced and give out third-hand knowledge which comes to them second-hand, or which has been passed down for many generations. Today men are still talking only from hearsay, seldom from true experience. They

97

are speaking from the knowledge and experiences of others. They tell of the works of the ancient apostles, of the founders of their creeds, even of Christ, without having fulfilled one promise He gave or having lived by any of the higher laws He revealed.

When each man shall have the power to "speak in the name of the Lord", he will no longer be occupied with dacadent, dead works such as those which shame the earth today. His works will be alive and filled with glory and he will be doing the works of power, which Christ designated to those who *believe*. And this power will not be an usurped authority of evil monopoly, which some have claimed in order to exalt themselves above their fellow men. It will be a power of complete knowing that will bring the fulfilling glory of Christ's Name into every man's life.

Anyone who becomes either bigoted, self-righteous or fanatical is one who worships a religion or church rather than God. Many groups are inclined to think they are the Lord's only anointed. Such beliefs shut out the rest of humanity and the great Fatherhood of God. Those who love God instead of a religion, church or sect, know of His divine love and glory in the great brotherhood of man.

This great, promised day when the divine brotherhood of all mankind is ushered in will be fulfilled just as soon as man himself permits it. This day of glory belongs to every man who will awaken to its reality and help to bring it forth.

This New Day will be established as man himself accepts the glorified Christ Light that has been given to abide within. As this Light is developed and becomes operative in Its unspeakable power to complete knowing, His Kingdom will be established on earth even as it now is in heaven—and earth will be heaven.

This divine Christ Light within man, when brought forth to its fulfillment of perfection, is LOVE completely glorified—love so pure, so compassionate, so divine and Christ-like it will go forth to heal a world. In this love all hates are healed, all fears cast out, all flesh transformed, all sins forgiven.

Down the centuries the Catholic church has carried, held out the symbol of this divine Christ Light unknowingly. Long since, however, it became only the empty symbol. Centuries ago the true meaning of the burning candle was lost in antiquity. Light a candle and let the burning flame lift your prayer up to the very ears of the Lord God of heaven. With a lighted candle the prayer is supposed to become a living essence which will reach unto His throne.

Light a candle on a Christmas tree as a symbol of the Divine Christ Light within. This is the meaning behind the lighted candles. But light a candle without thought or true understanding and it is only a brilliant decoration reflecting its gleaming light on many ornaments, which have only a momentary, worldly value. Light a candle without understanding and it remains but the empty symbol while the divine truth remains a concealed, forgotten, lost truth. Or turn on a hundred lights to reflect upon a thousand shimmering decorations and you still have only a lost symbol. Awake to the meaning of the symbol and realize that you are the candle from which His divine Light is to shine forth—and you will become that Light.

Know also that you have but to contact that inner flame of purifying glory by turning inward in complete surrender. Worship Him with all the strength of your own great, *unsealed,* open heart, melted in devotion and praise and you will not only be in contact but in tune with Christ.

His powers will become your powers as you begin to do the works which He did. You thus extend the Light which He holds.

Know that as that flame of Christ Light becomes a living glory of reality upon the altar of your own soul, all your requests will be instantly carried upon its releasing essence straight to the very throne of God. Thus will your prayers become the prayers of a "Saint and will ascend as incense unto the Lord."

You are the candle of eternal glory! But you may have remained unlighted throughout your entire life. Christ is the Light required to glorify the lives of men. Let His Light come forth from within! Let it shine out to give light to a world! Yea! Light it and feel the altar flame of His divine fire melt the seals within yourself! Light it and watch its glow expand as new vistas of eternal glory open to your view! Light it and by its increasing glory feel yourself cleansed and purified! Light it and watch it dispel the gloom and darkness of the centuries! Light it and by its unspeakable revelation comprehend all things! Light it and comprehend the great Truth as you step out beyond mortality to walk with God.

As that flame is lighted by your belief in It and guarded until you are completely filled with Its everlasting glory, you will become that Light for you will become one with It—and It with you. You are Its vehicle. Through you must that flame be sent forth. You are the lamp of Its expression. Through you It must be made manifest to a world. Thus you are the very tabernacle, the temple of God. Through you the great Christ Light must shine forth to heal and bless and help redeem a world.

Every burning candle in a cathedral, every lighted candle

on a Christmas tree, every beautiful light in the world is but the symbol of this divine Christ Light which is waiting to be released within your own soul.

From henceforth, whenever you stand breathless before gorgeous sparkling lights glowing in their splendor, know that they are only representing that which you were intended to be—and what you really are.

Light the candle in your own soul and you will never need to climb up any other way into the realm of higher vibrations. Light the candle in your own soul instead of in some church. Light that inner altar flame through love and praise and gratitude to God and feel the glory of His power flowing through you in its exquisite ecstasies of divine, eternal reality.

As you send love to Him with all your strength your strength will increase, for it increases with use, it becomes perfect with practice. With constant use your love and strength will grow and increase until your love will sweep the earth with its healing glory and enfold all in its heavenly peace, its infinite power of unspeakable, breathtaking beauty.

Love and pray with all the energy of your hearts and your prayers will become more powerful than the tempests and more dynamic than the deafening roar of many bombs. In your prayers will be contained the power to enfold the earth and hold it safe. In the power of such prayers your love will be exalted and increased a thousandfold. On the vibrations of your love-filled prayers the heavenly hosts will be able to reach through to dispel the powers of darkness. And, as you send out your love in this unselfish degree, it will increase until it will eventually vibrate across the Universe and play new melodies upon the very stars. This too is within your power and is to become your divine privilege as you fulfill all righteousness. As you send forth your glorified love upon the power of your prayers all darkness will begin to recede before you. Pray as often as you breathe and you will become the very glorified essence and power and light of your prayer. According to your faith and the power of your praying will the heavens be opened unto you and your powers increased and multiplied.

Love and praise and gratitude to God hold the keys of all power and all fulfillment, for these three are the living vibrations of the Christ Light released within you. Yea— "He who is thankful in all things shall be made glorious; and the things of this earth shall be added unto him an hundredfold; yea, more!"

As gratitude is released with love, it increases its volume and quality. And on the vibrations of man's own released praise and loving thanks the Light of Christ can be released to help heal and redeem a world.

If you have only a small crust of bread and send love and thanks to God for it, it will soon multiply into a loaf or into the equivalent of a loaf, for you will be using the divine law of multiplication, which is the law of increase. As you continue to be thankful, not taking any blessing for granted, your blessings will continue to increase. To the loaf will be added a supply of butter. As you go on in loving gratitude, praising God for His blessings, you open the very doors of heaven and that hundredfold will continue to increase, even as the widow's oil. As you send God love and thanks for each bounteous addition and increase, there will be no end to the supply. This is the law—His law of abundance. And it is every man's to use freely. It is power unspeakable.

If one plants ten kernels of corn he will reap a thousand.

As he plants that thousand he will receive a hundred thousand in return. So it is for each planting, for each glorified increase as one continues to offer his praise in loving gratitude. "He who is thankful in all things will be made glorious! And the things of this earth will be added unto him a hundredfold; yea, more!"

Anyone who sends out thanks continually in singing gratitude to God has, through that divine gift of inner appreciation, the power to close the doors on his fears, lacks and darkness. In this gratitude his lacks are destroyed and his self-pity banished into the "Nether Regions" from whence it came. When these things are overcome, one will of necessity become glorious, for he will be literally clothed in glory. Every vibration issuing from him will be in light, for he will have received; developed the power to overcome the darkness and this power will begin to extend beyond his own personal life in its universal healing of a world. This is not a childish "Pollyanna" theory contained in fiction. This is a law of God and its results are real and eternal. It is an irrevocable law and must be fulfilled unto him who loves and praises and sends forth his living vibrations of singing gratitude. These glorified vibrations, thus released from a human heart, contain power unspeakable and Light ineffable. These vibrations of everlasting glory and Light are first released through the body of him who sends them out. From there they go forth to enfold his loved ones, the world the universe.

If you would rise above drab, mortal living and become glorious, live the simple law of "being thankful in all things" as you send out your loving praise to Him who provides all things for your good. Never look at your lacks and your deficiencies and the things that are amiss in your life. See the crust of bread as a very blessing of life from God and give thanks for it. Give praise and blessings for whatsoever you have and it will begin to increase. This is the law of spiritual supply and multiplication. It is the eternal law of increase.

This is the law the widow used in multiplying the oil in her small cruse. This is the law Christ used in feeding the multitude. It is your law to use. You need only to grow into it.

First learn to multiply your own meager supply of inadequate blessings that they might become sufficient to fill all your needs. Bless and give thanks in all things.

After your own needs have been taken care of and you have learned to use the law, to change lack and poverty into blessings of plenty, then it can be used to provide for every need as it arises. With this divine law at your command you need no longer "Lay up treasures on earth where moth and rust doth corrupt and where thieves break through and steal." You will have laid up for yourself treasures in heaven, which treasures are the great spiritual powers of knowledge and understanding by which "All things can be added."

This law can and should be used constantly. Then one never takes any blessing for granted, never again becomes a dull, mediocre individual, for the very vibrations of glory are awakened within him and the Light of Christ becomes apparent. As that song of gratitude and love becomes a very part of one's being, so will the increased blessings and powers be as they come forth a hundredfold to fulfill the law.

This gratitude must be more than words. Words are only empty, meaningless little symbols that hold no power whatsoever when they are sent forth without being lighted as incense from that inner heart flame. Gratitude must be re-leased from the very heart center of the soul—the Christ center. When it is thus released it becomes a singing vibra-tion of infinite, eternal power. This inner, glorified vibra-tion of gratitude, sent forth in love and praise, is the vibration in which His Unspeakable Name is contained— the Name of All-power! Believe in that Name—and use it! This great, glorious vibration contains within it the Christ Light as it is released in awakened glory from the inner soul of man. It is the Light. It is the eternal glory and the power and the redeeming, exquisite Light of every man who will not reject it.

VIBRATION

Chapter VIII

There are many who die but never go to the "other side" at all. There is the "other side" and there is "this side" of the River of Life. The River of Life is the point of egress or demarcation into the Higher Realms. Those who are sin-bound and clothed in darkness are unable to cross that sacred River. They remain here, close to the earth, continually adding their evil and darkness to the already overburdened world. They inhabit the low places of iniquity, feeding on the evils and lusts of degenerate humanity. With all the despair of their own failures upon them and with the persuasiveness of their lusts burning and alive, they encourage mankind to sin, even as they sinned—and still desire to sin. Their own lusts are gratified in the transgressions of man. They even try to force others into their own degree of degeneracy if there are any who will give in to their subtle suggestions.

"For *we wrestle not against flesh and blood,* but against principalities, against powers, against the rulers of the darkness of this world, against spiritual wickedness in high places." (Eph. 6:12).

Those who have maintained any degree of their natural goodness cross that great River of Life and are placed in the realms of progress where they can be taught and reconditioned. Most of those of average, mortal standards

106

have as much unlearning to do as they have learning to acquire.

Everyone who has been overcome by the sins of the flesh and consequently death has much to learn—and much to unlearn, no matter who he is or what laurels he may wear. Those who die are the ones who "die in their sins." They are the ones who did not overcome while in the flesh.

It is in the flesh that the greatest opportunity of all existence is held. It is in the flesh, which is the divine crucible of God, that all evils can be most readily and permanently conquered. It is in the flesh that man stands upon the front lines of the great battle between the forces of Light and darkness. Every victory a man achieves in this life is for the benefit of all. And with each and every victorious degree of overcoming are eternal rewards and unspeakable glories.

No man's temptations are just his own. His temptations are also the temptations of all who have ever yielded to them or have been overcome by them. His victories are a triumphant release for all who have passed on through that portal of death, though the great reward is to him who does the overcoming. He who overcomes becomes "a co-heir with Christ" for this is the gift he left for a world, the strength of His own overcoming. This knowledge could be greatly enlarged upon, but there is neither time nor space in this record to do so.

This life is the time and place to overcome. Many who thought themselves to be perfect have the most difficult time of all in becoming readjusted and straightened out. Their sins may have been more of omission than of commission. They may not have broken any of the great laws, yet failed completely in fulfilling any of the higher ones.

They may never have felt compassion, radiated understanding love or been able to forgive any man a single error or mistake. They may have closed their eyes to the needs and wants of their fellowmen.

Hate, fanaticism, self-righteousness and every evil, selfish trait weave themselves into the very fibers of the soul and are most difficult to remove. All physical traits and weaknesses, accumulated in earth life, remain with each egressing soul. However, even the intention or desire to be or to do good makes progress a speedier, more enjoyable process.

Death is the way of correction, as stated in the book preceding this one, *Temple Of God*. It is a slow process of reformation that must take place gradually, as each individual is willing and able to bear higher teachings and greater light. Each man is his own gauge, even as he is on earth. His free-agency is always the deciding factor.

Those who die as martyrs, or those who give their lives in sacrifice as most of the soldiers have, are usually prepared to transcend many grades and degrees of ordinary, slower steps of advancement.

Those who take their own lives have been completely overcome by the powers of darkness and their position is quite tragic. It is most difficult for them to ever advance beyond their own point of highest thought patterns which they held during their earth lives.

There is no one waiting at the gates of death to herd the individual into some certain realm, some place of confinement, or to lift him into glory, as so many anticipate. It is entirely a condition of free-agency and preparedness. Each seeks his own level automatically. Those who are completely sin-bound and arrayed in darkness egress into their own level and degree of merit. They step into the exact conditions and vibrations they leave behind; or rather, it would be more exact to state that they take their vibrations with them. They are unable to behold the light or to discern in any measure the higher realms. Each seeks, even more readily than on the physical plane, his own kind and his own level.

Every selfish, evil trait of humanity carries its own vibration, which is plainly discernible in the spirit realm as color. Each individual carries an aura of color vibrations around him. These colors and vibrations are not discernible to the average mortal because man's physical eyes have not been conditioned to behold them as yet. There are sound vibrations that human ears cannot catch. There is the whistle used to call dogs that no human ear can hear. So are there color vibrations that do not register on mortal eyes. Every trait, be it good or evil, is registered as a color vibration in the aura of the individual and is plainly visible to those who are conditioned to see.

Every evil trait is apparent. Selfishness, pride, dishonesty, jealousy, hate and unjustness are plainly manifest. Those who have expressed nothing but their greeds and lusts are completely clothed in darkness.

Many are arrayed in vibrations of both light and dark, which, until clarified, only make a dingy, neutral, rather abstract indefiniteness as they merge without character or power. These are the ones mentioned in Revelations, the ones who, because they are neither hot nor cold, are very undesirable. They are not completely clothed in darkness, but the light they carry is defiled to the point of being unpleasant. And all who enter that gate of death carry some darkness and defilement with them.

Christ is the only One Who traveled the road of death

carrying no darkness whatsoever with Him. He was completely arrayed in all the glorious vibrations of triumphant overcoming. Death had no claim upon Him, nor has it any claim upon those who overcome. "Christ went beneath all things that He might rise above all things." And this does not mean that He went down into transgression and sin. Blameless and purified He went down into death, entering the realms which are beneath all things that He could open the doors of darkness and release the prisoners. (see I Peter 4:6).

"For Christ also hath once suffered for sins, the just for the unjust, that he might bring us to God, being put to death in the flesh, but quickened by the Spirit: By which also he went and preached unto the spirits in prison; which sometime were disobedient, when once the long-suffering of God waited in the days of Noah—" (I Peter 3:18-20).

The prison spoken of was the confining, vibrating darkness which each individual had taken with him and which had literally imprisoned and enslaved him. Christ, by His divine overcoming of sin, had the power to release the transgressors from their own vibrations, permitting them to view the light. And every individual who overcomes thus assists all who are wrapped in the darkness of their commissions and their omissions.

Christ had overcome all things and did not need to die, but in order to help redeem a world and those who had lived upon it prior to His advent, it was His desire to lay down His life for their redemption. But none, either before or since His time, have ever traveled that road of death without carrying with them the vibrations of their earthly errors, mistakes and weaknesses. Those who have overcome these things while in the flesh DO NOT DIE. Death has no claim upon them.

As human beings step through that portal of death, they leave nothing behind but their physical bodies and their worldly possessions. Every trait, every desire, every failing, weakness and thought vibration goes with them. Death changes no one, it exalts no one. It releases no man from himself or from what he really is.

If one's evil predominates over his good, then the dark vibrations defile the vibrations and colors of light until he is clothed in darkness.

If his good predominates, the Light vibrations can help to efface the tragic, ugly darkness of the evil vibrations to a great degree. It is possible that one may have overcome most of life's evils and has carried across with him only a few of his mortal frailties, which humanity takes for granted. Nevertheless, it was these very frailties and weaknesses that held him to the path of death and caused him to enter it. The little, insipid vibrations of mere mortal existence discolor the glorious, spiritual vibrations to a certain degree, no matter how mild they are.

Each person stands forth a revealed, complete record of all that he has been or even desired to be. There is no mistake, no misjudging, nor is there any condemnation. The love of God is still reaching out to reclaim and glorify all who are only willing. Those who are completely defiled take ages and eons longer to redeem or to release from the darkness; that is all. And for worlds without end they can never catch up with those who overcame in this life.

Next in glory and beauty to those who overcome are those who love so greatly they willingly lay down their lives for their friends. This love is the Christ love. It holds the power to release His Light so that individual is hailed into higher realms and can be speedily prepared for the highest glory. He who thus lays down his life because of a great love is next in power and status to him who overcomes. Overcoming is the highest.

Following him who gives his life because of the Christ love is the sacrificing in war of one's life to an ideal of truth and freedom to benefit a world. Those who hold the ideal of peace and freedom in their hearts, who are not fighting just for the sake of victory or to kill an enemy, are prepared for the next great advancement.

He who overcomes in this life is first and he need never die. He who lays down his life for a friend releases the Christ love within himself and so steps into higher realms. He who is sacrificed for the great ideal of *peace* for the world is third in preparedness and will be on the road of advancement.

Now, returning to mortality and its sins, immorality in any degree is one of the most corroding, retarding evils. It defiles more than any other transgression, except murder. It arrays one in the lowest of the animal vibrations. It is manifest as a dull, sickening vibration of an ugly, dark, depressing hue that holds the individual completely earth-bound, unless there are many good traits to offset and balance it in some measure. However, this is seldom the case, for an individual's good is usually destroyed very speedily by the animal vibrations of his evils, which he releases within himself, until they take over.

As sex desires are mastered and controlled one steps into a higher vibration and receives the color or raying light of majesty, though he may not realize it. This glorified ray of exquisite light is the first mark of evolving divinity.

No victory over the flesh is ever achieved that goes un-rewarded. No struggle is ever made that is not apparent. No victory is ever won without its being heralded by the individual receiving a vibration of light to signify that overcoming. And within each living ray of light is contained power to advance and to intensify each flame of glory.

This record goes beneath all things in order that it might assist man to comprehend all things, that he might rise above all things. Many of the human weaknesses have been listed here so the reality of vibrations may be understood and the path of overcoming be plainly manifest, that "all men might be left without excuse."

Uncontrolled tempers are only uncontrolled thoughts and emotions in full expression. Uncontrolled tempers are the violence of untempered individuals giving way to every evil vibration that touches them. By their very lack of control they use the strength of their divine energy to foster every evil, disintegrating vibration of violence in existence.

Every evil carries its own dismal, depressing color and its own disintegrating vibrations; and for every evil trait there is not only a definite color and tone but a power that is destructively negative. Each person is literally clothed in the color vibrations of his own thought processes as they have become the accepted pattern of his life. The thought actions have contained the seeds of all the manifest conditions of his mortal existence. These vibrations go across with him into eternity. Thus he is clothed in darkness or he is clothed in light, or any of the shades of dinginess in between, according to his own choice and free-agency.

As unbelief carries with it a veil of darkness, so does the power to believe carry with it a clear, penetrating blue ray of unspeakable glory. This blue ray is known as the "Christ Ray". It is not the complete Christ Light, but one of ITS rays, the most potent one. This Christ Ray is the ray of belief as it is developed into FAITH. As the divine Light of Christ is expanded and enlarged the blue ray completes and fulfills the ineffable power to actually KNOW. It is in the developing of this ray that God can be revealed and Christ become *known*. The blue ray is the most revealing, penetrating, healing ray in all existence. This blue Christ ray reveals and unfolds knowledge and truth so the individual can comprehend all things. It dispels ignorance and reveals clearly the exalted path of overcoming. And it is along this blue ray, as it is sent out to the very throne of God, that revelation is received. The blue ray is the ray of FAITH that becomes KNOWLEDGE. It is the Christ ray of truth and healing and unspeakable power. It is known as the *Faith* ray, for it is the highest of the Christ rays.

Beyond the white raiment is the vibrating glory of each individual's own developed traits of triumphant overcoming, as he leaves the darkness behind. Every virtue has its own color and place as it vibrates out in a glory of living light of throbbing, living emanations. Love, peace, joy, gratitude, compassion, honesty, virtue, brotherly kindness, truth and self-control each have their own glorifying, vibrating, living color. And these rays become an actual, eternal part of the individual who develops and wears them. Within each ray the color and vibration are added power and glory. And they are man's to use.

As one stands strong and firm against temptation, facing his life with courage, as he seeks to overcome, the vibration of living, liquid gold, the golden ray of overcoming becomes a divine reality. This ray is brought forth through praise and has power to dissolve the darkness. This golden ray is also one of the three potent Christ rays.

If one will but take his setbacks, his losses, his worries and failures and despairs and transmute them into light by accepting them, then praising and glorifying God for them, he can transform them into power and strength and infinite honor and perfection. As man uses this golden ray of praise, he releases the all-fulfilling vibrations and achieves a glory that is impossible to describe. This golden ray is the ray of transmutation, whether it be conditions, things or man's own self.

It is impossible to express these higher color vibrations of pure spirit in words simply because there are no words in any physical language to contain or portray them. They cannot possibly be described to those who are still on the mortal plane of existence. On the earth plane the few colors that do come through, excepting of course the sun's direct rays, are dead and lifeless. They are powerless and impotent, unless they are like the infra-red, violet ray and the few others which science has artificially produced. But even then man cannot look upon these artificially produced rays with his naked eye.

The lights and rays which are apparent to man's physical eyes are manifesting only on a dead world. On the higher planes of advancement the color vibrations are alive and eternal, with the essence of life's forces flowing out from them in everlasting power. They are entirely spiritual and are much more alive than the tangible neon lights of the present day, which are dreary and dead in comparison. The transmuting ray just mentioned is also the ray of translation. This ray of overcoming must be comprehended and perfected in order for one to achieve the final victory of exalting his physical being into the higher spiritual vibrations and life eternal.

In order for you to begin to comprehend fully the glory I am trying to share with you, I ask that you draw upon your imagination and use your God-given gift to BELIEVE, for the power of words is completely inadequate. The glory vibrating from him who overcomes is beyond all words and all languages. Only by man's ability to *believe,* which is the soul-exalting ability to *feel* rather than to see, can one begin to comprehend Truth.

As you begin to reach with your mind and imagination, using that awakened power to *believe,* you will begin your ascent into the realms of Light. *The ability to believe,* remember, is the blue Christ ray being accepted, developed and put into use. It is the revealing ray that holds naught but unfolding wonders in its penetrating, vibrating glory of unutterable power. In the blue penetrating ray of knowledge is the gift of inspiration and revelation opened to man. When that blue Christ ray of *belief* is developed and expanded, it is rayed forth direct to the throne of God and along that ray revelation and knowledge is poured back to the individual. It becomes an open window into heaven through which blessings are poured back to him who released it. Thus every developed ray becomes a channel of Light, glory and power. Revelation is the ability to know and comprehend great truths even before they become apparent, or before they have been proved.

Come with me and let the Light of Christ shine forth from within you. Come and use the great blue ray of His power. Yea, come! And doubt not! Doubts contain nothing but the defiling opposite of the glorious revealing ray.

Doubts contain the keys and the powers of eternal darkness which they foster on man.

By developing the power to *believe,* the blue Christ ray is touched and faith becomes established. "Faith promises all things, and it fulfills all things." As Faith fulfills all things it brings forth the complete knowledge, or the power to KNOW fully. This is the power to actually KNOW God.

However, before *knowledge* can come there must be the ability to *believe.* In the power to believe is the gift of faith held. *Belief* and *faith* are the enfolding ovum, or egg, in which the seed of *knowing* matures. No one can possibly *know* God or *know* of the greater spiritual issues unless he has developed the power to *believe.* As *belief* is warmed and nurtured it develops *faith*—and *faith becomes knowledge.* Knowledge is the point where the blue Christ ray is established in all its fulfilling power.

Any who begin to live the laws Christ gave will release the blue Christ ray into their lives and will pass beyond *belief* into the power of *faith.* Faith, as it matures, develops and transcends beyond the stage of *feeling* and becomes *knowing.* And *to know is to be able to DO!* Hence, "Knowledge is power!" In this are all promises fulfilled.

Follow faith, or the blue Christ ray through into the complete expanding glory of its power and the point of *knowing* will be opened unto you and with it will be given the power to receive the fulfilling of every promise ever given.

Now, to digress for a moment. Have you ever shaken hands with someone and felt an involuntary shudder go over you, followed by an intense desire to wash your hands thoroughly? This may happen even though the individual with whom you shook hands just emerged from a bath, so it is not a physical uncleanness which you desire to escape.

Then again, have you been in the presence of those who seemed to hold your respect and almost awed reverence, without your comprehending why? If you have experienced any of these things, you have been touched by the vibrations emanating from others and must of necessity *believe* in the reality of these vibrations or deny your own intelligence. Begin to use these powers of perception within yourself and develop them into *faith* and you will soon *know*.

The vibrations of light are the banners of glory flowing out from those who have achieved victories. These vibrations are the divine, eternal reality of spiritual existence.

The moment an individual catches a vision of the great issues involved and begins to use his divine gift of free-agency in choosing his road, from that moment he has stepped upon the path that leads upward, if he has chosen aright. Or, if he does not fully comprehend the issues involved but desires only to do the best he can, seeking to overcome his own inherent evils, he steps automatically into the path Christ indicated. But it is only as one completely comprehends the issues involved that he can fulfill all things in the great triumphant glory of complete overcoming. Hence these books have been written—for the time is at hand.

As one fulfills the higher laws the vibrations of light become an established part of his being. Before long his very presence will have power to dispel the darkness around him for he will be clothed in light. And that light is the living, vibrating essence of spiritual potency. As that light becomes completely established one is not only clothed in light; he actually becomes that light.

Every divine law fulfilled brings its own reward of glory and power. Every vibrating ray of glorified color is like a flaming sword, cutting away the mists and veils of darkness as it reaches up to the very throne of God.

Thus, as love is developed, hate, which is its opposite, is overcome and banished forever.

As the power to believe is developed the dark, enfolding veil of unbelief is rent and the blue Christ ray of faith and knowledge begins its outward reach of fulfilling glory.

As peace is brought forth within one's soul confusion, with its consequent errors and evils, is destroyed. In the gift of peace is contained the power of perfect manifestation in all things. Within the gift of peace is contained the divine fountain or pool of spirit which must become perfectly stilled in order that one's thoughts and desires may be reflected through to the spirit realm without any degree of distortion. With that liquid gold pool of Spirit completely stilled, through that gift of inner peace, the powers of creation are purified and perfected within the individual. This great peace is only achieved by learning to "Be still, and *know* that I Am God!"

As one begins to comprehend the powers of the Light of Christ, which is given to abide right within himself, he will desire that Light more than he will desire anything else in existence, hence he will desire only God's will to be done. God's will is that this Light be accepted and brought forth within each individual for his own everlasting, eternal glory and ineffable, exalted powers of godhood. Thus, only in the divine will of God is contained each man's happiness, glory, joy and perfection.

It is by and through the powers of the Light of Christ that all the keys of progress and development are released, even the complete powers of redemption and of overcoming. As the Christ Light is developed belief grows into faith, even as an infant grows into childhood. And faith grows into knowledge as naturally as a child grows into youth. Knowledge grows into power even as a youth begins to express manhood and stands forth to take his rightful place among men.

As one grows into this status of maturity, reaches this point of spiritual progress, he is ready to step forth from mortality into immortality. He who thus overcomes steps across time and eternity to enter the highest realms of Celestial glory without the dragging, painful processes of unlearning and learning being involved. He reaches the Highest by accepting the Light and becoming One with It. As he learns to walk with God in mortality, he will have the power to overcome death and stepping through the veils of both the darkness and the light, walk with God, or literally abide with Him forever. "To him that overcometh will I grant to sit with me in my throne, even as I also overcame, and am set down with my Father in his throne."

Death is the last enemy to be overcome. When pride, hate, lust, fear and all darkness and evils are conquered by glorifying and bringing forth the great Christ Light, death is banished.

Christ revealed the laws of the higher kingdom and the powers of overcoming death in these words: "He who will *live* the laws will *know*—". Few have believed in His teachings fully, so few have really believed in Him. Millions have professed their belief in words, yet none have proved that belief in deeds. Few have ever been willing to conform their lives to the standards He gave, nor have they been willing to travel the path He indicated.

"LIVE His laws and you will KNOW! *Live* His laws

and you will become like Him," for "You will be purified, even as He is pure!"

No one can even feebly attempt to travel His path without being benefited. No one can *literally travel* it without being glorified. And he who begins to travel *that path*, in determined gratitude for having found it, will have the power to fulfill all things as the evils drop away and all promises become living realities of eternal, exalted, unutterable power.

His road is for all humanity. None are excluded except those who exclude themselves. His realm is a realm of such unspeakable glory and power it could compare only to the most intense, glorious moments of happiness possible to experience in life, magnified and increased a million-fold, without ending, for it is that complete essence of exquisite joy established forever.

Progress is eternal. Stagnation is death. He who is satisfied with himself and with his earthly surroundings and mediocre conditions has ceased to progress—and where there is no progress death must ensue.

Many are not satisfied but their dissatisfaction is only expressed by giving vent to the negative impulses and violent dislikes as they spew out their wrath and anger in disintegrating, fault-finding vibrations of blatant discords. There are no constructive, helpful, healing vibrations or thoughts used by such; only the disintegrating forces of their own violence are released to add to the already overburdened confusion.

Those who are dissatisfied and use that dissatisfaction to find methods of remedy, or who reach up to God for answers, will be shown ways to help right the wrongs and purify the conditions.

Each shade and hue and color brought forth through overcoming is added power released in vibrating energy.

The "rose-colored glasses", spoken of by the poetic, are an actual reality. One beholds all conditions, all things, through a ray of rose-colored glory when he develops the gift of gratitude, which becomes a song of praising ecstasy and triumphant overcoming as it increases with use. This glorious, rose-colored ray has the power to transmute the hideous, dingy, brownish-red color of self-pity into its most exquisite spiritual banner of victorious overcoming as one becomes thankful in all things. This rose-colored hue of living can transform the evils of existence into multiplied blessings. This rose-colored ray is the ray of increase and spiritual multiplication. This divine ray is one of the three Christ rays and is most real. It is powerful beyond expression. As it is developed and intensified it becomes the living flame that can enlarge and glorify all conditions and things. It is the vibration released from the cross by Christ, who transformed the ugly aspect of the most disgraceful, ignominious experience in existence into unutterable glory and infinite, eternal power.

This rose-colored ray, or vibration, is developed through the gift of gratitude. As joy and gratitude are developed, self-pity and the powers of lack and failure are transmuted into unspeakable beauty and those who enter into this vibration truly become glorious! "He who is thankful in all things shall be made glorious; and the things of this earth shall be added unto him a hundred fold; yea, more."

The ray, or color of gratitude, is not exactly rose. It is only registered as rose-colored on physical eyes, when mortal beings have been lifted for a brief time into its enfolding glory. It is a deeper, more intense, more vivid ray

than rose. It is also one of the three Christ rays which are
so divinely potent and infinitely powerful and are contained within His Light.

The three Christ rays emanate through the great Christ
Light. The rose-colored or ruby-red ray has the power to
make one glorious. It is this ruby-red ray that holds the
power of multiplying all blessings for it is released through
gratitude. Praise and willingness to let God's will be done
releases the golden ray of overcoming and purification.
Belief and *faith* releases the divine Christ ray of penetrating
blue. This ray holds the keys of revelation and knowledge,
plus the powers of healing and the fulfilling of all one
can believe.

These three Christ rays contain all power and the perfection of complete fulfillment. Within these three heavenly, living rays, or vibrations, are contained all the relative
colors of the spectrum, beyond which is the great Christ
Light of concentrated *life.* As one contacts and brings forth
the Christ Light, all the vibrating, glorified rays of life
eternal become living powers. Every ray of the spectrum,
every hue of the rainbow is contained within the three
major Christ rays. Each ray is the symbol and the living
banner of some virtue and as they are developed and extended out from the individual, they become the avenues
along which all blessings flow to him from the very throne
of God. All the fulfilled and completed rays of the spectrum, which are the flowing banners of power and of overcoming, are contained in the great White Light of Christ
which is contained right within man.

It is utterly impossible to express this knowledge in any
clearer form at the present time. But it must begin to be
comprehended that these three divine, definite rays of in-

finite power and their related hues might begin to be expressed and brought forth to the point of complete, fulfilling power. Thus within the Light of Christ is contained all virtues and all powers. Only those who reject His Light because of ignorance or deliberate disbelief have remained destitute of these greater gifts. In the pure white Light of Christ is contained the three major rays of all power and all glory, with their related hues of vibrating virtues and ineffable glory. Because of ignorance, wickedness, slothfulness and dulled, stupefied acceptance of evil, the Light of Christ has been rejected and its blessings and powers have remained unknown. Because of man's rejection of the divine Christ Light, the whole world has remained under condemnation and unredeemed as it has continued in its gross darkness.

"Awake! put on thy shining garments, oh captive daughters of Zion!"

All the reality of the powers and the laws Christ developed and used He left behind for man to use also. They are all contained within the great Christ Light emplanted as a seed within the soul of man, waiting to be accepted and brought forth. As the three Christ rays are rayed forth from within the individual, all the other harmonious color vibrations of perfection and beauty will automatically be developed and will release their vibrating, celestial powers of perfection.

Truly, nothing is impossible! And all possible things are the results of the vibrations which enfold them as they are quickened and made alive in vibrating action. It is the power of Christ which makes alive all things, releases all vibrations of light and glory in living power, transforming their opposite negative, dark counter-poles of evil into infinite Light. Christ's power and Light has the efficacy to completely spiritualize and redeem the dark, negative forces and transmute or transform them into infinite effulgence and unending, dynamic, eternal force.

Man stands at the very center of these colors and glorious vibrational rays of living light and power and their opposite hues of disintegrating evil, until he uses his free-agency to follow his own inclinations for either good or evil. Within man is the ability to balance those colors, to overcome all the forces and powers of darkness. It is for each man to say which he will choose. And each man actually becomes those vibrations which he elects as his choice. If he elects the higher, he becomes elect. He only is elect who chooses to follow the Light and who loves God with all his entire being. He who rejects the Christ Light degenerates into the darkness.

All the dark vibrations and their consequent evils can be transformed into vibrations of power and divine light as they are touched and enfolded in the expanding Christ Light. And for every dark, dingy, repellent color and vibration of evil there is its glorified, spiritualized counterpole of reality contained within His Light.

Humility is a flaming banner of brilliant, dynamic power that is exquisitely beautiful. Pride and its every aspect are the complete opposite, both in color and vibration. Pride is one of the most difficult of all evils to detect on the physical plane, though it is one of the most retarding. Included in pride is self-righteousness, self-seeking, the habit of falsifying and exaggerating along with most dishonest procedures. Pride is bereft of real love and of all brotherly kindness. It wishes to be loved but cannot bestow it.

Love carries its own vibrations of breath-taking beauty

which intermingle and blend with all others, enhancing, intensifying and glorifying them into greater beauty and power. When love is perfected the darkness and fears are overcome and their corresponding virtues are brought forth. When this divine love is developed until one fulfills that first and greatest of all commandments and loves God with all his being, his intelligence and strength, he is truly entering the point of divine power. When the love for God is carried another step farther to enfold the race of men in its embrace, it contains the substance of all good in its everlasting embodiment and unites with Celestial powers. In this love there is the power to heal, to bless and to redeem. All the darkness will be conquered as Christ's Light is thus released from within. The singing vibration of praise and thanksgiving and love IS the Light of Christ as it is rayed out in flowing glory. Within the perfect love is also contained the ineffable powers of the Almighty, as praise and gratitude find their own avenues of expression in singing melody. This is the great new song that will wing its way to the very throne of God. This is the song of the righteous which none can learn except those who *live* the higher laws. It is the *living* of the laws that produces righteousness and all the fulfilling powers thereof. As one takes upon himself the glorifying vibrations of the Christ Light he actually becomes that Light, for it becomes established within him. And all evils melt before it and are consumed.

It is as simple and easy as that. Develop that dynamic, inner song of joyous praise and love and gratitude. Let it become the rhythm of your soul, the pulse-beat of your existence, for in it no discordant, negative thought or feeling can either enter or go out from you. When these three intensified, glorious Christ vibrations are expressed within your own soul, you will hold the very keys of eternity in your hands. With this perfected vibration of His Light it will not be necessary to linger or to look back at the evils, for they will be dissolved and their effects forever healed.

I invite you to come with me. Step out upon the vibrations of pure Light and view the breathtaking wonders of eternity. Rend the veil of darkness, which is only the darkness of your own unbelief and its accompanying evils, and step across the dark abyss of death into Celestial realms. On the higher planes there are no discords, no hates, no negatives, no evils or darkness, no errors or mistakes, for these things are overcome. As you step across into the higher vibrations of glorified living life, you will help to lift the whole world with you.

Every gift and power Christ held in His hands while in the flesh, He left behind for man to use. He marked the path, revealed the laws and showed the way. Then, to leave no gift or power unshared He gave His Light to abide in every man who cometh into the world. He also left His peace behind, for all who would only desire and accept it. In seeking for that inner peace, "Which peace is beyond thought", because it is contained in the feelings, man will discover the great Light and Its unspeakable, ineffable powers of fulfilling glory. He left the record of all that He was—and IS—and what man can become. "—And lo, I am with you always, even unto the end of the world. Amen." He is with every individual who has ever come into the world. And when man no longer rejects that Light of Christ his redemption will be fulfilled and the vibrations and powers of darkness will be released and dissolved. His powers are but awaiting man's acceptance of them.

This is the reason those who reject the Light of Christ are under condemnation. Instead of sending out the glorified Light of living rays and infinite power those rays are reversed. Their dingy, evil counter-parts of negative decadence are being slowly turned inward with devastating effects. The individual is being attacked and bombarded with every evil thought and emotion and trait he creates and those disintegrating vibrations begin their work of destruction within his own being. From this reverse condition comes illness, old age, senility—and death.

The laws are exact and unfailing. Only in the Light of Christ is contained the powers of man's redemption and exaltation.

THE RAINBOW

(A supplement to Chapter VIII)

The covenant of the rainbow is an eternal covenant. God Himself established it and set it in the sky as an everlasting witness to man that the world would never again be destroyed by a flood.

There are many types of floods besides water. There are overwhelming floods of vicissitudes, disasters, heartbreaks, pain, trials and sorrows. And man is constantly being destroyed by such floods because he has not comprehended the fullness of that glowing symbol in the sky or lived up to his part of all that the covenant implies.

There is a legend as old as the rainbow. It is in every land and among all peoples. It is the story that if one can reach the foot of the rainbow he will find a pot of gold. This ancient legend is based upon divine truth, as are most legends. The ancient saying has lived throughout the centuries, though spoken with a smile as man shrugs his shoulders in a wistful wishing which is instantly dissolved in a sophisticated, adult, unbelieving amusement that discards fairy tales and a belief in Santa Claus. And man does not realize that he has lost the path of power and fulfilling truth because of his drab, unbelieving attitude.

This ancient legend of the pot of gold that accompanies the rainbow cannot die. It is truth and is eternal and as beautiful and glamorous as the rainbow itself. Man has not comprehended the truth behind the symbol of the ancient legend. Nevertheless, no human being has ever beheld a rainbow without being lifted, for a moment at least, into a warmth of enfolding pleasure, though he may be completely unaware of the true meaning of it and only remotely touched by that tingling vibrating of hope.

Even the animals feel pleasure in the rainbow. There is a secret rejoicing and a voice of peace whispered into the consciousness of every living thing as God's promise is reaffirmed. Those rainbow colors are a symbol of the diffused Light of God flowing out as though through His own encircling arms, to bless the whole world. And there is a vibrating response from the souls of all that lives.

And now, it is of the legend of the pot of gold that I would speak. No one has gone through life without having stood at some time at the foot of that rainbow—and knew it not. Whenever you have stood in the rain with the sun suddenly shimmering through the clouds, you were standing at the foot of the rainbow. From some place in the distance you were standing on the exact spot where that rainbow ended.

You laugh and say the legend is a lie, for you found no pot of gold. You were perhaps unaware of the fact that you were at the rainbow's end, nor did you understand the glory of the truth behind the symbol or the legend. That pot of gold is real. And it is "the gold that has been tried in the fire." It is the pure gold. And he who possesses that gold is rich indeed.

It is in the intermingling of the rain and the sunshine that the rainbow appears and that rainbow is the symbol of an eternal covenant between God and man. And with that symbol lives a legend of a pot of gold which contains an everlasting promise of every good thing, to those who seek to know the truth.

When the storms of life submerge one in floods of sorrows, troubles, vicissitudes, heartbreaks and calamities that only tears can release, let the tears flow freely. Tears, like rain, have a cleansing and purifying power that helps to give life to hard-baked, barren soil, whether it be the earth or a man's own hardened heart. Welcome those tears, if they are not of weak self-pity, and through the tears lift your eyes to God and let a smile come through the clouds of your dismaying despair. As that smile of sunshine mingles with the tears, say something on this order and mean it: "It is all right, dear God! Everything is all right! I love You! And now I accept Thy Will and ask only that it be done in all things! Let this condition be glorified to You! Let it be transmuted into honor and power! And praise and thanks and glory be to Thee forever and forever! So be it, Father!"

That smile must come through the clouds of despair as caressing and love-filled as the sunshine through the rain. If you can say the foregoing and mean it, you will have the power to reveal the glory of the rainbow in its fullness. You will in that instant be raying out the sublime, radiant hues of all the divine virtues contained within you. You will be raying out the divine Light of Christ from within as it is diffused into its glorified beams of color, which contact the very throne of God, instantly and without restraint. At the foot of those radiant rays is the center of your own soul, the Light of Christ, the chalice of pure Spirit, the pot of gold contained within your own divine soul-center. And within that pot of gold, of Spirit, is the sacred pool or mirror of infinite, all-fulfilling power. Into that divine pool of Spirit you can image-in your pure desires, your needs, your holy requests and they will be rayed out along that rainbow of glory to the very throne of God. It is in this manner all noble and divine requests are brought into complete fruition within your life. It is not for you to meddle in how they are to be brought to pass. The Christ Light within makes the complete manifestation possible as God does His works through It. You are the cup, the chalice in which that divine gold of Spirit, the Light of Christ, is contained. You are the reality behind the symbol. It is only as you comprehend that you can claim that pot of gold and ray out the hews of the rainbow in your own desired virtues to bring the fulfillment of God's full covenant into reality within your life.

This cauldron of gold contains the divine riches of God! This is the true wealth! This is the gift of God as His power flows forth into action to end the floods of adversities and bring the harvest of abundance and innumerable blessings into manifestation right within your life.

This divine gold of the Spirit is the means by which every material, desired blessing is brought into being and becomes manifest.

As one learns to transmute his sorrows, expressed in tears, in this manner the great triumphant song of gratitude and praising love releases those divine powers within. Thus the Light of Christ is released in Its fullness and is rayed out in the diversified colors of glory and virtue to the very throne of God. This is a covenant God established with man and it cannot be broken. When man sends forth those rays of glory from his own Christ-center they must receive attention and be answered instantly. Along these radiant, living colors the cosmic rays of God's fulfilling, completing powers spring into action and that individual's life must receive the blessings.

This is the full and complete meaning of the covenant of God's rainbow—the covenant between God and man, as He established it centuries ago. It has stood for ages. It will remain forever. It is entirely up to man whether he will avail himself of its blessings or be submerged and destroyed by the floods of life's many adversities. But for him who accepts that covenant and fulfills his part of it, there is no flood or disaster on earth which can overwhelm him. Neither can such a one be touched by earthly circumstances, except in blessing. He who lives by the covenant of the rainbow walks with God.

Beloved, glorious one, if you comprehend these eternal truths you will learn of their infinite powers. You will not need either the floods or the tears to reveal the rainbow. That rainbow and its eternal covenant are henceforth yours to ray out to the very throne of God in all the perfecting vibrations of unutterable glory as they are released from within you. You will have complete access to that divine pool of Spirit through which all desires are brought to pass. It too becomes your everlasting possession.

Use these laws in holiness and you will be using them according to their right-use and nothing will be impossible to you.

Chapter IX

"And if your eye be single to my glory, your whole bodies shall be filled with light, and there shall be no darkness in you: and that body which is filled with light comprehendeth all things.

"Therefore, sanctify yourselves, that your minds become single to God, and the *days* will come that you shall see him: for he will unveil his face unto you, and it shall be in his own time, and in his own way, and according to his own will.

"Remember the great and last promise which I have made unto you; cast away your idle thoughts and your excess of laughter far from you."

The greatest, crowning, last and highest promise of all promises is that man shall behold the face of God. As man learns to control his thoughts, using them correctly and with comprehension of their power, they will no longer be idle. Neither will one who thus has control of his thinking processes need to indulge in the pastime of those who are both empty and foolish, usually displayed in an excess of laughter.

God does not sanctify any man. The command is and has always been: *"Sanctify yourselves."* This sanctification can only come through one developing eyes single to the glory of God. As one begins to purify himself by correct thinking processes and by developing the gift of love to the extent that he begins to fulfill that first and greatest of all commandments, his eyes do become single to the glory of God, for he begins to receive the higher vision of God's enfolding glory and of His power. God's glory is everywhere! It is in the sun and the moon and the stars! It is in the rose and in the tree! It is in every blade of grass and in the morning dew! It is in the rain and in the splendor and immensity of the sea and the sky! It is in the song of a bird! It is also in the heart of man!

"The earth rolls upon her wings, and the sun giveth his light by day, and the moon giveth her light by night, and the stars also give their light, as they roll upon their wings in their glory, in the midst of the power of God.

"Unto what shall I liken these kingdoms, that ye may understand?

"Behold, all these are kingdoms, and any man who hath seen any of the least of these hath seen God moving in his majesty and power.

"I say unto you, he hath seen him: nevertheless, he who came unto his own was not comprehended.

"The light shineth in darkness, and the darkness comprehendeth it not. Nevertheless, the day shall come when you shall comprehend even God, being quickened in him and by him.

"Then shall you know that you have seen me, that I am, and that I am the true light that is in you, and that you are in me, otherwise ye could not abound!"

Man has gone through life with his mental and spiritual eyes completely closed. He has "had eyes to see, and seen not." He has taken everything for granted, without thought or appreciation, without joy, gratitude or understanding and without that awakened, marveling vision of wonder.

He has not opened his mind to comprehend that back of all existing and created things stands the divine Creator. The spiritual feeling of awe and reverence is "the fear of the Lord" mentioned so often in the scriptures. This old Anglo Saxon word "fear" meant "awe". To be in "awe" one's attention must be focused upon God, must contemplate His wonders. And he who does so will be held in spellbound, marveling adoration.

As one begins to use his wandering, idle thoughts to think upon these higher things, he will develop the power to comprehend and to enjoy more fully and more completely everything his eyes behold, until in a glory of enfolding love and singing gratitude his eyes will of necessity become single to God's glory. At first it will be a mental awakening, as his understanding is opened and his comprehension expanded to feel the wonder and glory of all that is. It will be an inner vision of awakening that will unfold into the full light of *knowing*.

As one begins to comprehend the power and the wonder of that divine Christ Light, he will outgrow all negative thinking, which thinking contains all the darkened powers which have created each man's ills and misfortunes. As he casts out every negative thought and feeling, "The darkness will be cast from him." . . . . . "And there will be no darkness in him: and that body which is filled with light comprehendeth all things" . . . . . "even God!"

In referring back to the first quotation, it states: "And the *days* will come that you shall see him;" Any scripture, at any time or in any place, which refers to "day" or "days" is speaking of something concerning this earth. "Days" is a measure of "time". On the other side, "time is not". With this explanation it must be understood this unveiling of

His face is something that is to take place in this life. It will be when the individual prepares for it and it will be when the individual fulfills the laws concerning it. It does not say "day" but "days" and means that after that revelation one will be able to behold the face of God the remainder of his days. This is the point where one receives "the fullness of the Father!" This Fullness of the Father is an eternal gift. It is not just given for a moment or even a day, but when it is fulfilled it is forever, for one then enters another, higher dimension.

After one has learned to cast out the darkness and the negatives, a process which intensifies the gift of appreciation and joy, he *must* be filled with light. With all the negatives and evils eliminated, there is nothing left but the great light. No individual can possibly remain a vacuum. He either has to be filled with the light or the darkness, or with their intermingling vibrations. If he is filled with light there can be no darkness in him. This great light is the power to comprehend all things. It also contains the joy of be-ing. It is the very glory and power of God. With this understanding one's eyes soon become single to the great glory. They no longer behold the darkness, the evils of life and their consequent powers of negation. When this is completed the final step must follow. It is then the greatest, most glorious and last promise must be fulfilled, even the unveiling of the face of God.

"For he will unveil his face unto you, and it shall be in his own time, and in his own way, and according to his own will." How else could it possibly be done? Could a rose unfold before its time of maturity? And if it did, would it be beautiful? Could it come forth in any other way than His way? Remember that no man can create a rose, giving it color and fragrance and loveliness and life. Each and every rose, in order to fill the measure of its creation, must come forth in His time. And His time is always when the rose has reached, or fulfilled, the measure of its unfolding.

It is the same with the chick in the egg. Its time of stepping forth into another plane and dimension is God's own time and that time is when the chick is ready.

This great revelation that is to unveil the Face of God to the individual who is ready is also to be done in His own way. That, again, is the only possible way it could be done. His way is the way that has arranged all the laws which govern such a divine and ineffable revelation. His way is the process of developing and unfolding from within until the required perfection is attained. No rose could possibly come forth in its completed loveliness by enforced measures of outside prodding and interfering. The rose itself has to be ready—and, shall we say, willing?—even as an individual has to be ready. That preparedness can only be accomplished through man's cooperation and complete willingness.

As God unveils His face to an individual it is always according to His own will. This is the only perfect way for it to be accomplished. And be it here known, it is always according to God's will that this great, unspeakable revelation of Himself is vouchsafed to man. It is always God's will for this to happen. It is His will for all things to come forth in their fullness and beauty and complete expression. It is always His will that every child of His reaches that status of maturity and purification in which the great revelation can be fulfilled unto him. As man receives the fulfilling perfection and is able to receive "that great, and last promise", his own mortal destiny is completed. In this unspeakable revelation of God is contained all the powers of eternity. Death will be overcome and all the ancient dreads connected with it.

This has always been the will of God for every man who has ever come into this world, so when that final promise is fulfilled it will most certainly be according to His will. It has always been His will that this be accomplished. It is only as man begins to use his gift of free-agency aright, in awakened cooperation, that God's will can be completed and fulfilled in the life of man.

Always the great blessing of fulfilling any law is to the individual who fulfills it. If one adores and worships God, it is that individual who advances as the fountains of love are opened up in his own heart to release the very power and life force of God right within himself. If one fulfills the commandments and the laws of righteousness, it is to himself the joys of the Almighty flow back in breathtaking glory. Whatever man may think he is doing for God he himself is the real beneficiary.

God needs no man's adherence or devotion, except to be used for the redemption and glorification of that individual. Each precious gift and ray of light and devotion offered is but an avenue through which unspeakable powers and blessings are poured back to the one who released them, multiplied, increased and glorified a thousandfold; yea, more.

For God has said, "This is my work and my glory, to bring to pass the immortality and eternal life of man." But it must be when man is *willing* and begins to cooperate.

"Cast your bread upon the waters and after many days it will return unto you." Cast your thoughts, your devotion and your love out upon that universal sea of God's vast expansion and they will return unto you laden with blessings. If you are waiting idly, impotently, negatively for "your ship to come in", realize that you have sent the wrong kind of ship to the wrong port. The sea of God's great abundance and the power of fulfillment of all good for you are but awaiting the sending of your ship to the proper port in the specified way. And your ship will come back to you laden with all the precious, divine gifts and blessings will be poured out upon you without measure, for it is His good pleasure to bless those who love and serve Him. And this is His great desire for all as He continues in His work of "bringing to pass the immortality and eternal life of man." Included in this work is your own complete redemption and eternal glory laden with every good gift that is possible to receive, if you will only lift your eyes to behold such glory—even the glory of God. Eyes single to His glory is a condition attained by a purified state of continual, conscious awareness.

There are those who try to bully and threaten God, or who seek to make picayunish little deals with Him. "God, if you don't give me this or that or the other, I will never pray again!" Or it may be this threat, "I will never go to church again!" So what? Such an individual is only inflicting the loss of that divine contact with God upon himself. No one can possibly spite or injure God. The individual alone is injured as he separates himself more completely from God and His great healing, enfolding light. Or there are those who pray thus: "God, if you will give me this or that or the other, I will do this or that for you." No one can do anything for God, for whatever he does for God he is but doing for himself and the reward will be his own.

There is not anything that can possibly happen to any individual on this earth that will not be turned into a blessing if that person will only accept it as a gift from God and humbly glorify Him and give thanks. Yes. This does mean even your heartbreaks, distresses, vicissitudes, losses and sorrows. Bless them and praise God and they will be clothed in glory and transmuted into power and blessings to you forever. The greater the sorrow the greater can be its released power as it is transformed into a radiance of infinite potency.

When Christ prayed, "Father, if it be possible, let this cup pass from me. Nevertheless, let not my will, but thine be done," He gave the keys of all glory. And with that inner love released He later proclaimed in great joy, "Now is the Father glorified in the Son." With His eyes wholly single to the glory of God He achieved the greatest victory possible for Himself—and for God—and for a world.

When an individual can lift his vision to the great glory of God and have his eyes single to that Glory, he will not even pray for "this or that or the other." He will worship and adore and love with a devotion that will vibrate across the Universe in such a rhythm of power all things will be fulfilled in him. "And the things of this earth will be added unto him a hundredfold; yea, more!" . . . . . "And he will be made glorious."

Don't try to make deals with God unless you always give Him the biggest end of the bargain. And if you will just give Him your all without any bargaining, in utter and complete surrender, there will be no way to estimate your gains.

Glorify Him with every breath and become glorious. Give thanks and praise to Him for what you have and watch your "little" grow into "much". Your blessings will increase as by a miracle. Let your eyes become single to His glory, as you shut out the negatives, the fears and the darkness and you will be prepared to behold His face—and will be filled with His fullness, even His glory.

Love so much that whatever He sends will be as a very rare and precious gift. Love and adore, praise and give thanks and the windows of heaven will be opened unto you and you will not have room enough to receive the blessings.

"Therefore I say unto you, all things, whatsoever you ask when ye pray, believe that you shall receive; and they shall come unto you.

"And when you shall kneel to pray, forgive, if you have aught against any man; that your Father also, who is in heaven, may forgive you your sins."

As you love and worship and adore God, your very requests will be in tune with His Will and His Holy Spirit of Promise will bear witness to your soul that you shall receive them. Learn to listen for that assurance—and believe it always. As you learn to believe in that inner assurance the blessings will follow. That is His law—the law by which all requests are granted. Anything you ask for in this manner, fulfilling this law of prayer and learning to hear His promise will be granted unto you. If you ask amiss and the prayer is not for His glory or for your own ultimate good or for the good of him you might be praying for, that desire will be removed from your heart, if you yield yourself to His wisdom and to His will as you pray in this manner.

If you pray that your little child be spared *and it isn't,* you may be sure there is a very good reason. Perhaps God, in His infinite mercy and love, is saving your precious child from some teenage tragedy later. Your child is His child too. It was His long before it was yours. Why not trust Him in handling the affairs of life and death?

Or if you pray, without yielding your will to His will, that your husband or wife or sister or brother, your sweetheart or some other loved one be spared and they are because of your refusal to relinquish that loved one, then such a life is usually taken later with much more suffering and anguish attached. There are thousands upon thousands of cases to substantiate this truth. And the great extended misery was created by your unyielding. It was actually created by your personal will being placed above the will of God. It was not His doing, nor was the added suffering required. Nor was He trying to add extra punishment.

It is possible and it is the will of God that all pain and suffering—and death be overcome. But death can only be overcome by overcoming its cause, which is sin. It is not overcome through self assertion or by defiance or by exerting one's own will above the will of God. Death is overcome by obedience to every beautiful, divine law and by yielding to God's will in a love of praising gratitude that completely fulfills all laws, hence has the power to banish death. Use this method and you can pass from death into life. Fulfill the higher laws and you will also be able to lift your loved ones so they too will be able to comprehend His glory. They too will be able to lift their eyes to His heights and receive the vision divine and the blessings thereof.

Until one accepts and lives by the laws that fulfill the full measure of creation and hence have power to overcome death, it is a help to comprehend that for every loss there is a divine compensation, if one will only receive the gifts of the Holy Comforter.

"For it is given to abide in you: the Comforter; the peaceable things of immortal glory;" etc. For every sorrow there is ample comfort and the power of complete healing. Within every loss and every searing heartbreak there are also contained the ineffable powers of advancement, progress, redemption and glory. All the greater things are accomplished by overcoming the small things through love and praise and gratitude, and by developing the ability to accept all things, all conditions as though they were His will. In this attitude they can be instantly exalted into blessings and the greater laws will automatically be fulfilled. Thus can one be exalted and glorified.

In the Will of God is contained only the ultimate happiness and the power to perfectly work out all evil conditions. Man sees it not because man's vision does not extend beyond the present hour—the present day. If one will lift his vision to the glory of God, whose scope views all eternity, and accepts His will, he will have power to walk with God! He will no longer need to drag along keeping step with time. He will be in step with eternity and will be enfolded in eternal glory.

In the Will of God is contained all the glory and the power of the ages. In His mind and will is the perfect working out of every problem, the healing of every pain, the relief for every sorrow, the righting of every wrong and the perfecting of every imperfect condition.

It is not necessary to make deals with God. It is only necessary to tell Him of your problems and ask for His help. Then let love and gratitude pour out from you in songs of everlasting praise for a privilege so divine—and all things will work together for your good—for your glory.

So many are lost in the great vortex of engulfing, heartbreaking difficulties because they are continually battling against life and every condition that unfolds. They battle events, their fellowmen and life itself. There is only one fight for any man to really make. Man's only important battle is to subdue the "self". As it is overcome all evils go with it. When this is accepted man will be able to relax in the great tide of God's flowing current of life and in that relaxing love and praise he will be lifted high upon the crest of the stream of life, instead of being completely submerged beneath it. He will be carried almost effortlessly into the great ocean of His abundance and peace and completeness of all things and receive the fullness of joy.

There is no need to spend one's life battling the currents in a little, unimportant eddy, unprogressive, unglorified and unredeemed by a lifetime of wasted, unproductive living.

"Be still! And *know* that I Am God!" Let your troubled heart be still and His healing and His comfort will flow in. Let your troubled mind be at peace and lift your eyes to His glory, for in His glory is the exalted redemption and joy and perfection of all that He created. And His creations are always perfect. He created nothing except beauty and perfection and love, happiness and eternal joy. It is only man's interferences and negative creations of discords and evils and violence that are so terribly devastating and completely destructive. Lift your eyes to His glory and let His will be done in all things and the great perfection will ensue in your own life. Your life will be filled with it. Only you and others like you can bring the fulfilling of the prayer, "Thy will be done on earth even as it is in heaven."

Cease "Kicking against the pricks!"

As you learn to worship and adore and give thanks to Him continually you will lose the power to ask amiss and your prayers will be the unfolding of His will in your life as you are prepared to receive blessing after blessing, truth upon truth, glory upon glory until you are prepared to behold His face and receive of His Fullness.

Let only love go out from you in a singing glory of praise and gratitude. In so doing you will not need to spend your fragile, impotent strength battling to fulfill your will and bring the universe into tune with you. You will become in tune with the Universe. And with the great stillness now at your command you will walk with God. Your eyes will become single to His glory. And as they become adjusted to behold that great, divine glory, He will unveil His face unto you. In such intimate, exalted understanding you will truly be prepared to receive of "The Fullness of the Father!"

There is nothing in all existence that can surpass a glory so great, a goal so complete and a joy so all-inclusive as one puts off mortality and puts on immortality—even Eternal Life. Henceforth such a one will actually *know* God! "For this is life eternal to *know* Thee, the only true and Living God, and Jesus Christ, Whom You have sent!" With eyes single to this glory, such glory can be fulfilled in every man who will only lift his eyes to behold it.

THE KEYS OF THE HIGHER REALM

Chapter X

To the rich young man who had kept all the earthly laws and desired to know what else he could do, Christ said, "If thou wilt be perfect, go and sell that thou hast, and give to the poor, and thou shalt have treasures in heaven: and come follow me." In these words Christ gave the method by which one can completely detach himself from the hold and bondage of physical possessions. It is not the individual, as a rule, who possesses either money or things. It is the physical belongings which possess the individual.

In St. Paul's inspired words on Charity, he states, "Though I speak with the tongue of men and of angels, and have not charity, I am become as sounding brass, or a tinkling cymbal.

"And though I have the gift of prophecy, and understand all mysteries, and all knowledge; and though I have all faith, so that I would remove mountains and have not charity, I am nothing.

"And though I bestow all my goods to feed the poor, and though I give my body to be burned, and have not charity, it profiteth me nothing."

If the rich young man had taken Christ's suggestion and sold all that he possessed and given to the poor he would not have completed the law of perfection unless he had turned from the things he released and followed Christ.

Anyone who gives out alms or donates to charities, who helps to clothe the naked or feed the hungry or does any

147

other act which he boasts of later, has accomplished very little. Any man who boasts, who even mentions any good he has ever done is not following Christ at all, but is serving the world and is seeking its rewards. He who gives must follow the admonition, "Let not thy left hand know what thy right hand doeth: that thine alms may be in secret; and thy Father which seeth in secret himself shall reward thee openly."

If one gave away all that he possessed, even to a great fortune, and later lived in the memory of the act or even held it in his thoughts, he would still be clinging mentally to all that he gave. Such a one has not really given at all, for he is still holding to it with his mind. He could not possibly be free from his gifts in such a case. As soon as anything is given it must be released completely from the mind of him who gives.

There are those who have given away fortunes, but they carry the memory of those fortunes with them. They remember always that they gave this man so much and that one so much—and so on. Or they donate certain amounts to charities or organizations or what have you and do it for the sake of praise or appreciation and hence lose the real reward.

To remember any gift that has been given is but holding on to the things one professed to give. And there are those who give great gifts to posterity and have their acts remembered by suggesting some memorial. To such their earthly monuments contain the reward for their actions.

Every kind act, every exerted ounce of energy given in some service to the world or whatever works one performs for others must be immediately forgotten, lest in holding to the memory one has not given at all but is retaining to himself the gift.

If such a one should tell even his left hand what his right hand has done he is claiming the reward for his gifts, his acts, in seeking worldly credits and mortal appreciation. And in doing so, he has received his reward.

If, on the other hand, one gives all that he has to give as though he were only the steward and it were a divine responsibility, a privilege to dispense the gifts of God to those in need, then turned his mind and heart to follow fully the path Christ indicated as he sought to bring forth that divine Christ Light, he would find that already he was holding It in his hands. And in that gift he would receive the very riches of heaven. The riches of heaven are the ineffable powers of God as one comprehends them and becomes powerful in that *knowing*. One's meager little worldly contributions, though they amounted to millions, would be as nothing in comparison to gifts and powers so great and reward so divine.

The reward or credit for any good which one may do is instantly dissipated and destroyed by the telling. Such acts and donations are entirely between God and the giver— and the receiver. It is only in the heart of the receiver that the gift and the gratitude for it must be kept alive. The giver's heart must let go of it. His mind must realize it— and never must his act be profaned by his telling it.

Anything that is given, which the giver constantly recalls to mind, has not been given at all. He is still claiming the gift as he seeks, perhaps unconsciously, to receive the reward or worldly credit.

Give whenever there is an opportunity to give. Share your little and know that it is a privilege to share. Every opportunity you lose in helping or giving is an opportunity lost to you forever. It may only appear for an instant and then be forever withdrawn.

Or it may be that you meet the same beggar every day of your life. If that is so rejoice, for to you is given the rare privilege of sharing your more abundant life with him. If you have aught to give it is only required that you share a little of your blessings with him. Remember, the beggar has to live today, and tomorrow—and the next day, the same as you have to live them. Because you ate yesterday is no reason why you do not need to eat today. The beggar needs to eat also. Forget the coin you gave yesterday, even as you have forgotten the meals you ate.

Give without any thought of credit or reward. Give for the sake of giving and for the privilege of having something to share with God, "For that which you doeth unto the least of these, my brethren, you do it unto me." Be grateful for the opportunity to prove to Him that you appreciate the gifts and blessings He has so graciously bestowed upon you. If your store is small, bless and give thanks as you give, then go your way praising God that you could share and your blessings will begin to multiply. And remember always that it is far greater to share your little, give something you could use or even need, than it is to give something that you do not require for your own comfort and well-being.

"And Jesus sat over against the treasury, and beheld how the people cast money into the treasury: and many that were rich cast in much.

"And there came a certain poor widow, and she threw in two mites, which make a farthing.

"And he called unto him his disciples, and saith unto

them, Verily I say unto you, That this poor widow hath cast more in, than all they which have cast into the treasury:

"For all they did cast in of their abundance; but she of her want did cast in all that she had, even all her living."

This is just a tender example of the great and mighty things that can find expression through a human heart.

The laws governing the higher realm are ignored because mortal eyes have not been lifted to behold their divine beauty. Man has not even attempted to live them because he has been satisfied with the lesser, ugly laws of the flesh. He has been satisfied with the laws of vengeance, of "dog eat dog" and selfishness and greed. He has been satisfied only because he has not comprehended the glory of the higher things or caught the vision of laws so breathtakingly sacred and so divine in their ineffable powers of perfection.

"Whosoever shall smite thee on thy right cheek, turn to him the other also.

"And if any man will sue thee at the law, and take away thy coat, let him have thy cloak also.

"And whosoever shall compel thee to go a mile, go with him twain.

"Give to him that asketh thee (and the asking may be an unspoken appeal. It may be only a tin cup extended, or a hungry look reaching out to you in misery), and from him that would borrow of thee turn not thou away." (Even if you know the article or amount borrowed will never be returned, it is much better for you to lose the article or the money that it would be for you to deny the request. And it is also better for you to be the loser of such possessions than it is for the individual who would keep them. Bless him in his blindness and release that which is borrowed from your mind. In this way you will be completely freed both from your physical possessions possessing you and from any resentments over your losses. Just send out love and praise and step beyond the shackling bondage of mortality.)

"Ye have heard that it hath been said, Thou shalt love thy neighbor, and hate thine enemy.

"But I say unto you, Love your enemies, bless them that curse you, do good to them that hate you, and pray for them which despitefully use you, and persecute you;

"That you may be the children of your Father which is in heaven—"

If you think it is an indication of weakness to live laws so completely out of harmony with earth's standards it is because you have never *lived* them.

Any who abide by these laws are not weak for these are the laws of another kingdom—the kingdom that is not of this world. These are the laws of infinite power. These are the immutable laws of eternity—and of God. And they are yours to live.

And when you begin to fulfill them see that you tell it not. The only way these higher laws can become a part of your life and your life become a part of a higher vibrational order is for them to become an automatic performance, not a burden; not something to boast about, not a source of resentment or of self-righteousness. They must be performed as naturally as your resentful, discordant, negative thoughts and actions are performed today.

Live these higher laws and you will know. Live them without any thought of being righteous, without a desire for either credit or reward. Live them naturally, for they are the natural laws of the higher kingdom—that is not of this world. No one who abides in the higher realm would conceive of living by lesser laws. Nor would any individual in that higher realm think of bragging about living those simple, natural laws of the spirit any more than a mortal would think of bragging that he had obeyed the traffic signal on the corner of Times Square, or that he had fulfilled his normal everyday assignments of ordinary living.

If it is difficult for you to give and share and more difficult for you to let go of things without telling about your sacrifices, then for the time being forget about sharing your worldly gifts and blessings. There is one thing that you can give that will increase with your giving. Give love. Give love to God and to every human being. Send it out in prayers for every living soul. Pray for the world and every individual upon it. Pray and love and give praise continually. This service is difficult to boast about and love increases with every tiny shared vibration of its released glory. Soon you will understand how to live all the laws of the higher kingdom and will be able to pass into it.

Continue to pour out love to the world if you think the higher laws mentioned in the first part of this chapter, the ones which Christ gave, are too difficult. Give love and soon you will discover that you have the power to fulfill all the laws—for you will automatically fulfill them as your fountains of everlasting love open wide to pour out the great Christ Light to enfold and help heal a world.

Share yourself by giving love and you will soon be sharing all that you possess in a new-found joy. You will glory in a more extended vision and abide in a hitherto unknown happiness and power. Love perfectly and you will evolve into the kingdom to which all the higher laws pertain. Love and you cannot help serving as you are admitted into the vast Brotherhood of Light. And as you are welcomed into this higher realm of eternal progress, you will have power to help usher in the great New Day which is at hand. Then will you know that you are indeed a child of your divine Father which is in heaven. You will know of His love for you and bask in that love.

Keep in mind that any service rendered in whatsoever capacity and then boasted of, even shared casually, has received its reward in a lower dimension and the supreme joy of being lifted, or exalted, into a higher vibration has been cancelled. Anyone who boasts or brags about anything he has ever done closes his own door into the higher realms. He has stopped his own progress as he has placed a mediocre tag upon himself. He has only proved that he is still an inferior being, clothed in mortality. He is still earthbound and is only struggling to obtain a seat to be seen of men. Such has claimed his reward from the world of men instead of obtaining it from God. He has been willing to accept a menial's pay. He is not a son, but a servant.

WHAT IS RIGHTEOUSNESS?

Chapter XI

There are some who think that righteousness is in beards, in the length or heaviness of one's whiskers. Some think it is contained in long hair; some in drab, ugly, colorless apparel, not realizing that God created the gorgeous coloring of the butterflies and the birds and the flowers, the sunsets and the rainbows. God created all things to be as beautiful as possible. He never intended women to hide their beauty behind little, beetle-like costumes of drab dreariness. Beautiful apparel only becomes detrimental when it is used to satisfy one's empty vanity. It is then one realizes that every good can revert to evil if permitted to be carried to excess. It is in excess that the good can be transformed into ill.

Some think that righteousness is contained in everything that is unprogressive and backward, either in the physical, mental or spiritual realms. The old ways, unrelieved by modern inventions and comforts, do not have a monopoly upon righteousness. Every invention was brought forth to help lift the original curse of man, that he might no longer have to earn his bread by the sweat of his brow. Everything that is helping to lift that curse is of God, for the day is at hand.

The glories of heaven are only possible to manifest through eons and ages of advancement in every line of endeavor. Those who reject the beauties and comforts of

155

this world, thinking they are serving God, know nothing about God nor of His righteousness. Neither do they comprehend the beauty He has created to be expressed in all things. God expresses His greatness always through Love and through beauty. Those who turn their backs upon beauty and the new and wonderful, progressive things are in no way prepared to step into the wonders of eternity. Holding to ugliness and to old, dead ways does not prepare one for eternity. It only places seals upon such that may take ages to remove after death has finally released them from their folly.

The only danger in beauty, luxuries, comforts and lovely apparel is that man is apt to set his heart upon the outward show and hence loses the permanent values of all that is perfect and divine. It is possible that a woman can work so hard to clothe her body perfectly she will leave her soul naked and ashamed. The physical body is only the more apparent in this little span of mortal life. The Spirit is that which is apparent throughout all eternity.

If one does not permit the things of the world to take possession of him, but rather, uses them rightly, makes the right use of them, then he is beginning to comprehend righteousness. He will then accept all of the marvelous gifts, which God has bestowed for the pleasure and joy and comfort of man, with a true sense of appreciation and gratitude. He will use all things for both his physical and spiritual advancement in a balance of love that will glorify God always.

Some shun movies and television as instruments of evil. They are often used for evil, but behind these inventions is a means of instruction that all ages of the world have unconsciously waited and hoped for. When these means are used to portray all that is lovely and wonderful they will fulfill the divine purpose of their coming forth—and that time is very close at hand. When the movies and television are used to honestly and truthfully reveal the struggles of individuals, groups or nations in their endeavors to over-come adversities and to reveal their triumphant victories, they are but giving the world a divine glimpse into the conditions and the sacred achievements of mortality and revealing the goodness of God in action.

Righteousness is not contained in backward styles of hair-dos, beards, clothing, or in a lack of enjoyment of all with which God has blessed the earth. These backward ideas are retrogressive and unenlightened ways of self-righteousness, which carries its ugliness out into the open to be seen of men.

Righteousness is contained in the human heart. It is in the thinking and feeling attributes of man. It is expressed in love, gentleness, long-suffering, patience, brotherly-kind-ness and in that vibrant essence of inner praise and rejoic-ing that is released to God in eternal vibrations of loving gratitude.

Righteousness is not something that is worn as a garb to be seen of men. Righteousness is worn on the inside as the innermost reality of the love-filled soul of man. It is worn thus until it eventually fills every cell and fiber of the individual and he becomes *IT*. Then it is that he will be filled with Light—even the Light of Jesus Christ—and he will be clothed in that Light and in its glory.

This clothing is so beautiful and so far above anything even "Solomon, in all his glory" ever possessed, there is no Comparison.

Ugliness, dreariness of mind, drab, ungainly clothing or

a lack of colors have no part in righteousness. These carry but the outside manifestations of the grim dinginess of that which has seeped through from the Nether Regions.

Glorify God through love, praise and gratitude and you will become glorious, will be clothed in glory. This song of joy and appreciation is righteousness in full expression. This supreme gift of gratitude and singing praise and love alone is pleasing to God. This alone is God-like.

Any outside display of apparel, style or action that is worn to be seen of men is only a show of self-righteousness and is completely without value. It is not spiritual adorn-ment. It is an erroneous idea that spiritual beauty must be expressed in an ugly physical cloak. That which is spiritual is manifest in its own way and likeness, which is in ex-quisite beauty.

Righteousness is something that must be *lived*, not *worn*. It is something within, not something displayed on the out-side. In the humble, glorified perfecting of true righteous-ness, man becomes that righteousness and it has nothing whatsoever to do with fanatical conformities of clothing, styles, drabness, ugliness or backward unprogressiveness. All that is spiritual is expressed in loveliness and beauty and joy, in adoring praise and gratitude and loving worship.

Righteousness is the "right use" of all the manifest beauty, the spiritual perfection, the supreme love, the prais-ing glory of devotion and thanksgiving that wings its way heavenward in a song of eternal joy. Righteousness is not only the "right use" of the spiritual powers and beauty locked within a man's own soul, but it is also a releasing of all the spiritual strength and love and light as it is permitted to flow back to the throne of God, increased and glorified. Ugliness, drabness, deadness, dreariness, unprogressiveness or mortal, physical conformity has nothing whatsoever to do with righteousness.

Righteousness is the releasing of all the spiritual powers and strength of men in the great, triumphant achievement of divine overcoming.

Righteousness is not a rejection of all that is beautiful and lovely. Righteousness is the "right use" of all the blessings and powers of earth and of eternity. He who becomes the slave of the things of the world is misusing them and his own inherent powers. The things of the earth become misused instead of being used rightly as divine blessings from God.

As one learns to use the tangible gifts and blessings correctly, he will be prepared to comprehend and apply the spiritual powers of eternity.

One has to make the right use of his heart, his soul and his mind in expanding his divine faculties to encompass that Kingdom of God and the wonders of heaven. The Kingdom of God is not revealed or comprehended in narrowing down one's vision and faculties, but in the enlarging and expanding of them until one's mind can begin, in a measure, to encompass the wonders of eternity and the glory of God.

When man begins to comprehend and to make the right use of all things, including the things of this earth and of all his divine faculties of love, appreciation and understanding, he will be prepared to become a resident of the Kingdom of Heaven, for he will be exalted to the status of son-hood. It is here that all things will be added unto him which will enhance his well-being and his comfort and his joy. It is here that he will get a growing comprehension of the nearness of God and the ineffable use of his powers.

When one is admitted into the great order of the Brotherhood of Light, or becomes a member of the Church of the First Born by having brought forth that divine, holy Light of Christ until It fills his whole being, or until he is filled with Light and comprehends all things, then he is prepared to have Christ, or the divine Light, reveal the Father.

Righteousness is a song in the soul, a devotion in the heart, a gratitude of praising thanks expressed in a joy of love.

Righteousness is as free and unhampered as the color and fragrance and beauty of a flower. It is as spontaneous and effortless as the song of the bird. It is as unrestricted and immense as the sea, as boundless and all-enfolding as the sky.

Righteousness is not a cramped, restricted way of living and feeling and thinking. Righteousness is the great inner, released glory of a man's own soul expressing itself in every glorified act of bounteous, beautiful living.

Righteousness is a condition that has left the mortal fears, negatives, dislikes and discords behind. Righteousness is devoid of pride or self-seeking. It is a condition of love so pure, so free and so all-inclusive it comprehends all things, even the souls of men and their needs.

Righteousness is not achieved through striving or skimping or cramping one's thoughts, nor in a denial and rejection of God's beauty and glory as it gathers to itself only drab ugliness. Righteousness is as beautiful as the blossoms, as divine as the Light of heaven and as powerful as the symphony of the universe, for it is a part of that glorified symphony in expression as it is manifest in the soul of man. Righteousness is all that is beautiful, good, lovely and divine.

Glorify God in songs of everlasting praise. Worship in an adoration beyond words that are expressed in pure happiness and inner joy. Worship in an adoration that becomes an expressive part of the great, eternal symphony of God's glory. Let your soul awake to His power and His perfection and His glory until your eyes and mind are filled with naught else—and you will be righteous.

As you walk thus with Him, clothed in the immortal power of His great, enfolding love, the world will feel that righteousness and seek it for its own.

Righteousness is not expressed in a long, sanctimonious face or in drab ugliness, either of clothing or surroundings. Neither is it expressed in fanatical condemnation for all who do not fit into the mold you may have constructed for yourself, no matter how rigid that mold may be. The mold you are locked in may only be your own ugly, self-constructed cocoon, as you lie spiritually dormant and unproductive of color or beauty or loveliness and without power to soar into the heights, where spiritual vision is perfected.

It is not righteousness to try to fit another into the pattern you have selected and constructed for yourself. Your neighbor, friend or family member must be permitted to glorify God in his or her own way and according to his or her own vision and understanding. This is your own righteousness in action as you permit all to use the great, divine gift of free-agency which God has so generously bestowed upon all.

Love much! Rejoice always and forever! Sing your inner songs of praise and thanks and you will be letting your own light so shine that others, seeing the glory of it, will also seek to glorify God by setting their own light aglow.

The great spiritual song locked within a man's soul, when

released in its triumphant soaring of love and praise and gratitude, is the pure, undefiled righteousness of God in full expression.

Righteousness is not a thing of ugly, drab, conformed restriction.

Righteousness is the inner song of your own soul as it is released freely into the universe as your part of the eternal, divine symphony of heaven. It is the expression of your own love and praise, joy and gratitude singing from within in expanding, spiritual glory.

Whenever that praising song of happiness, of joy and gratitude is released from within, you may be sure you are in tune with the infinite. You are more—you are a very part of heaven's symphony. As your own song of eternal light and glorious righteousness is released to assist in mingling its own melody with the divine symphony of heaven being sung at the throne of God, you become one of that group of chosen ones. This is righteousness. This is the beauty of God in full expression in your own wonderful, lovely life.

BORN OF GOD

Chapter XII

Before one is born of the flesh his body is enfolded in complete darkness. At birth the infant comes forth into another dimension of light, growth and activity in which the seven physical senses are developed and the instructive period of progress in a mortal world is established. Babies are completely helpless at birth because they have to learn how to manage and handle these bodies of flesh and bone and to develop their physical senses, through which all earthly knowledge and information is obtained. In being born of the flesh, the infant is placed in an environment where it can mature physically. It is also endowed with all the divine equipment with which it can mature spiritually if so directed, or if it so chooses as it reaches the age of accountability.

It is usually when one becomes dissatisfied with the material world and its heartbreaking disappointments, with one's physical surroundings that his spiritual growth commences, if he uses the dissatisfaction aright. It is when one begins to yearn to *know God* that progress really begins. This yearning is the most intense longing within man, yet he knows it not. This spiritual, inner longing is much more intense, though intangible, than is one's hunger for food.

There is no need or desire of man's that was not provided for, if man is only willing to cooperate. The Spiritual hunger is appeased in the fulfilling of the following promises: "Seek me early and you shall find me!" Or, "Seek me diligently and you shall find me!" That eternal promise of finding is proclaimed aloud in these divine words: "Ask and it shall be given. Seek and you shall find. Knock and it shall be opened unto you. For *everyone* that asketh receives. And he who seeks finds. And to him who knocks it shall be opened."

This great, Spiritual longing is a divine hunger stirring within man. It is a spiritual hunger demanding appeasement. It is a hunger more real than the hunger for food, or the physical desire of sex, or for any earthly thing. It is the hunger of the soul, that cries from within, which the human race is striving to silence through the acquisition of wealth, property, fame or any of the desperate, grabbing acquisitions in which modern man is engaged. That hungry cry has often been silenced in the physical being of man because his "ears to hear" have been stopped up by his physical senses taking over to the point of sensuality. "And from that time forth man became carnal, sensual and devilish."

It is impossible for any human being to focus his attention upon that urgent, spiritual desire within without learning to "ask, seek and knock" and hence receive the great feasting which was promised. This feasting is on the hidden, or spiritual, manna. As the soul begins to partake of this hidden manna, or food, it speedily grows into its full maturity.

No individual develops to the point of personal revelation until he begins to "Ask, seek and knock", until he begins to desire to *know* God and is willing to discard all preconceived ideas and orthodox teachings in order to permit Christ to reveal the Father. "All things are delivered unto me of my Father: and no man knoweth the Son, but the Father; neither knoweth any man the Father, save the Son, and he to whomsoever the Son will reveal him." (Matt. 11:27).

Only in this advanced Spiritual stage of desiring to *know for oneself* is it possible to reach the point where one can be born of the Spirit. One must reach the point where he is no longer satisfied with a diet of "second-hand food". He must reach the point where he insists upon his food being "first-hand". Then only can he be taught of God. Then only can he be born of God, or of the Spirit. "That which is born of the flesh is flesh. And that which is born of the Spirit is spirit."

"Now there was a man of the Pharisees, named Nicodemus, a ruler of the Jews: The same came to Jesus by night, and saith unto him, Rabbi, we know that thou are a teacher come from God; for no one can do these miracles that thou doest, except God be with him.

"Jesus answered and said unto him, 'Verily, Verily, I say unto thee, Except one be born again he cannot see the kingdom of God'.

"Nicodemus saith unto him, 'How can a man be born when he is old? Can he enter a second time into his mother's womb and be born?'

"Jesus answered, 'Verily, Verily, I say unto thee, Except one be born of the water and the Spirit, he cannot enter into the kingdom of God. That which is born of the flesh is flesh; and that which is born of the Spirit is spirit. Marvel not that I said unto thee, Ye must be born again. The wind bloweth where it listeth, and thou hearest the sound thereof, but canst not tell whence it cometh, or whither it goeth: so is every one that is born of the Spirit'." (John 3:1-8).

The above states clearly that those who are born of the Spirit will have the power to come and go, even as the wind, and that none (who are still in mortality) will know where they came from, or where they go when they depart.

There is so much truth contained in the above quotation it will be necessary to approach it from several angles in order to make it fully comprehensible and to explain this Spiritual birth which is indicated.

An egg is the symbol of creation. It has always been the symbol of creation. It is used also in most ancient lands as the symbol of the Creator.

An egg is born of the chicken. Within the egg, which holds the symbol of potential life, is the embryonic chick. *The chick is born of the egg.* Whenever the maturing bird reaches the point of development as far as possible within the egg, it must come forth into a new world *or perish.* It must, by its own efforts and inborn, instinctive intelligence, begin to exert itself in a greater way than it has ever before known. It must begin to struggle in its intensified effort to overcome. The enfolding walls have to be torn asunder. If the chick only makes an opening in the shell large enough to get a glimpse of the new, greater world—the world of another dimension—without continuing its efforts to completely free itself, it still has not accomplished its intended destiny.

Many individuals only advance far enough to behold the higher vision in their minds but never go on to fulfill it. If the chick stops its progress at this stage it dies. If man ceases here, he also will be claimed by death.

There is another point which must be comprehended. After the chick comes forth from the egg it can never again return to its cramped, enfolding walls of darkness. Neither

can the individual. For such there is only the great freedom.

The same is true of the caterpillar encased in its cocoon.
Within the dense, confining, silken web of darkness the
worm develops wings and flaming colors of beauty. It develops strength and vision and finally reaches the measure
of its progress when it must break its enfolding walls and
emerge—or die. No outside tearing away of that embalm-
ing, silken enclosure can be of any help. It has to be rent
from within, even as the shell of the egg has to be broken
from within. This inside effort is most necessary that the
butterfly might develop wings to soar and the chick to walk.
The rending of the cocoon must be accomplished by the
crawling worm as it progresses into another phase of its
existence. It must be when the worm is completely prepared and ready. It must prove its readiness by releasing
itself. When the worm has fulfilled the laws of its own
being and qualifies itself by its own infinite struggle and
efforts, it can come forth a new creature. In that development it leaves the worm stage of its existence and enters a
new dimension where it can soar above the fields and
flowers. It no longer crawls on its belly in the dust. And
never again can it return into its prison of enfolding darkness. It is free!

The same laws are true of the bird, of the rosebud as it
breaks its sepal covering, of the acorn as it bursts its outer
shell of confining darkness and takes hold of the light,
and true of man as he purifies himself and by his own inner efforts releases himself from the binding shackles of
earth.

All things that so reach forth into a new dimension of
progress never again return to the imprisonment of their

former condition and existence. No man enters a second time into his mother's womb to receive his great spiritual release. That which is born of the mother's flesh is flesh. "Mother earth" is the physical mother of all material existence and of all earthly elements, of which mortal bodies are composed.

But that which is born of the Father is spirit. To be born of the Father is the new, spiritual birth which is required. This birth is quite different from the physical birth, yet in some ways it is quite similar.

Every human being is imprisoned within his own qualified, restricted self and its environment. Oh, he may travel and explore. He may have many acquaintances and activities, even as the worm. Nevertheless, he is imprisoned within his personal self—a creature of earth. He is of the flesh. All mortal beings are of the flesh. They are still confined within the darkness of their restricted, unenlightened, uncomprehending, mortal consciousness. They behold through the eyes of flesh "darkly". They work through the faculties of the flesh whether they be *professed* prophets, beggars, or kings. Mortal man is restricted and is a third-dimensional being. All the wealth, physical possessions, worldly honors and earthly knowledge will not break man's enfolding shell, or make him other than what his own physical conception holds forth—a mere mortal being.

Man's existence is a third-dimensional condition and though he has not realized it, it is in a dark and dreary world that he abides. He has little or no spiritual vision, for he has not developed his spiritual *eyes to see*. He is spiritually blind and is enfolded in darkness. And unless each man begins to exert himself and struggles for his own personal release—he will die—even as the chick in the egg will die unless it makes the effort to free itself.

No man has the power to release another from his physical, enfolding walls. Each man must catch the vision and begin the struggle for his own freedom.

"Everyone who asks receives; and he who seeks finds; and to him who knocks it shall be opened," even the door to a new and glorified dimension. Such a one, as he who makes that divine struggle for himself, will be born of the Spirit and will no longer be of the flesh. He will be able to come and go "As the wind and no (mortal) man will know where he came from or whither he goeth", not any more than a crawling caterpillar will comprehend the comings and goings of the butterfly.

The chick had to do so much developing within the egg, the rosebud within the calyx, the worm within the cocoon and man within his fleshly body.

This physical life is man's state of worm consciousness, compared to that which is ahead, if man will only fulfill the laws of his own progress. This work is given to reveal fully the great issues involved.

When man begins to develop by spiritual expansion, which power is contained in an awakening attitude of understanding, he will be able to reach the measure of progress where he can break the seal of "self", of flesh, and being born of the Spirit, step forth into a new and higher dimension. This higher phase of existence is as far above the present state as the butterfly is above the worm, the chick beyond the egg, the rosebud beyond the green, enfolding sepal.

How is it done?

First, by an awakening of the desires to the extent of

spiritual asking and an awareness of that inner longing. It is commenced by developing the spiritual faculty and power to *believe*. As one begins to *believe*, hence to hope and to aspire, he naturally begins to grow into the new Spiritual unfolding that is required for release. As long as he is satisfied with what he already believes and knows, as long as he sealed in any orthodox conformity of passivity, or is willing to be led by those who are themselves blind, there is no chance for him to emerge into the greater freedom and comprehend the divine truth—to *know* God.

When one reaches the point where the spirit grows into the fullness of the physical confines and surpasses it, that outer shell of mortal crust will have to crumble and give way. It is then one begins to see through his spiritual eyes and hear through his spiritual ears, to comprehend through his spiritual understanding as he steps beyond mortal, physical functioning. The point where the spirit grows into the fullness of the physical being is when all promises begin to be fulfilled, all powers begin to be bestowed, all truth becomes comprehended. When the spirit catches up with the physical, there can never again be any material want.

Below are listed a few of the teachings of John, the Beloved, which reveal the ways of achievement.

"God is Light, and in him is no darkness at all." (I John 1:15).

"He that saith, I know him, and keepeth not his commandments, is a liar, and the truth is not in him. But whoso keepeth his word, in him verily is the love of God perfected: whereby know we that we are in him. He that saith he abideth in him ought himself also to walk, even as he walked." (I John 2:4-6).

"He that saith he is in the light, and hateth his brother,

is in darkness even until now. He that loveth his brother abideth in the light, and there is none occasion of stumbling in him. But he that hateth his brother is in darkness, and walketh in darkness, and knoweth not whither he goeth, because that darkness hath blinded his eyes." (I John 2:9-11).

"Love not the world, neither the things that are in the world. If any man love the world, the love of the Father is not in him. For all that is in the world, the lust of the flesh, and the lust of the eyes, and the pride of life, is not of the Father, but is of the world." (I John 2:15-16).

"If ye know that he is righteous, ye know that everyone that doeth righteousness is born of him." (I John 2:29). "Little children, let no man deceive you: he that doeth righteousness is righteous, even as he is righteous." (I John 3:7).

"Whosoever is born of God doth not commit sin; for his seed remaineth in him: and he cannot sin, because he is born of God. In this the children of God are manifest, and the children of the devil; whosoever doeth not righteousness is not of God, neither he that loveth not his brother." (I John 3:9-10).

"Beloved, let us love one another: for love is of God; and everyone that loveth is born of God, and knoweth God." (I John 4:7).

Again: praise and love and gratitude are the most dynamic of all powers in developing and bringing forth that divine Light of Christ until it fills one's entire being.

The inspired, beloved writer of *The Odes of Solomon,* which are contained in the Lost Books of the Bible, when telling of his own translation has this information to give: "—And great was I among the praising ones." Any individual upon this earth can *become great among the praising ones.* Praise is an essence released from the soul of man. It is increased with use and becomes potent with power. It has the efficacy and the power to reach to the throne of God instantly. This praise of infinite glory is not the praise of empty words spoken aloud in blasphemous phrases, proclaimed in public places. This is that inner song of loving devotion and singing gratitude which ascends from the soul to be heard only by the ears of God. This is the adoration that is beyond words. It is born of the innermost *feelings* of man and no words have power to express it. As one's praise of loving gratitude is thus released to the very throne of God, that individual will soon be exalted to that very glory. This praise is sent out from the heart, the soul and the mind to fulfill that greatest of all commandments. It is love in its highest expression. The releasing of this inner praise contains the preparation necessary for the spiritual birth.

Praise and love and gratitude hold the keys to the great Christ door—the door of the new birth. "Behold, I stand at the door, and knock: if any man hear my voice, and open the door, I will come in to him, and will feast with him, and he with me." That Christ door is the door into another dimension—another phase of glorified existence. It is the door of "overcoming".

"I have overcome the world!" declared Christ. Man can also overcome the world. But he must overcome it through bringing forth that Christ Light from within until it fills the little mortal shell of "self". The Christ Light must fill his mind, his soul and every cell and fiber of his entire being. When that is accomplished the mortal prison of the flesh will have to give way and one will truly be born of the Spirit. Before he reaches this point of complete renewal, or the full rebirth, he must develop into his maturity by living according to the laws of spiritual development. He must begin to live spiritually, partaking of the Spiritual food, the hidden manna.

The Spiritual food is most easily reached through prayer which is exalted to the state of loving praise and gratitude. This symphonic prayer ascends from the very center of a man's soul and is the New Song mentioned in Revelations. This divine center is the point of the great spiritual stillness. It is the place where one can "Be Still and *know* that I am God!" Even as one's supply of physical sustenance is provided by the mother's milk in the beginning, so is the spiritual supply of hidden manna provided by the Father as one grows into the Fullness of the Father. "Be Still and *know*" and partake of the Father's inner supply of soul nourishment and spiritual food.

The infant first becomes aware of its mother through her providing the food to appease its hunger. This is how the child first *knows* its mother. When one receives of the higher spiritual nourishment in the stillness of his own soul, he partakes of the hidden manna of the Father, the food which will help him grow into his spiritual maturity.

When a child reaches the advanced stage beyond infancy where the earthly father supplies the food, it is then necessary that it begin to exert itself in its effort to partake of that food. The child must sit up and learn to feed itself. It is true that the food is supplied by the father, but the child must make theeffort to do the eating. So it is when an individual advances to the state where his hungering and thirsting after righteousness prepare him to receive of the hidden manna, the spiritual food provided by the Heavenly Father.

"Be still and *know* that I am God!" holds the keys. An infant, in order to partake of its nourishment, must first become "still". This "stillness" is not the stillness of sleep. It is the stillness of concentrated alertness. Man, in order to partake of the spiritual food, the manna of God, must also become "still" in a new sense of awakened awareness. This divine food of inner, hidden manna is "The bread of life", which Christ promised. In fact, He stated emphatically that He Himself was that "'Bread of Life". And it is most certainly true. This inner, hidden food that is so necessary for the feeding of the soul is the Light of Christ. Man must begin to comprehend its supply of unending power and grow into his own ability to partake of it. As one grows quiet and still in a love of praise and inner gratitude, he will learn the source of his divine supply—and as he partakes of it he will grow into the *knowledge* of God.

"Blessed is he who hungers and thirsts after righteousness, for he shall be filled"—with the fullness of God.

The stillness spoken of is only attained as one learns to go within the temple of himself, humble and love-filled. He must enter these sacred precincts reverently and with a tender gratitude of devotion that opens the very doors of glory at his approach. In this way only is it possible for him to enter the "holy of holies" in the very center of his own soul as he leaves his mortal thoughts and feelings on the outside. This "holy of holies" is the place of inner stillness—"the secret place of the Most High"—where one finds his own contact with God.

In this divine, inner contact one is led fully to the great Christ Light. He is not only willing to abide by the higher laws; he is grateful for the privilege. And with an awakened vision and intensified desire, he begins to conform his new life to the great truths and principles of a more advanced world. He receives the key to the great Christ door.

As one learns to enter this stillness of his own soul, he finds that all the clamoring of the little mortal "self" is silenced and the power of God takes over. It is in this divine silence that the great powers of God become operative in a man's life and all things begin to work together for his good—and his full development.

It is in this inner stillness that the Will of God begins the perfecting of His work. Within the Will of God is the complete and utter fulfillment of all that is beautiful, perfect and divine. There is nothing in the Will of God that is not for the joy and glory of the individual.

The Will of the Father is first contacted through learning to believe in that divine Christ Light which has been given to abide right within each and every man who has ever come into the world. "This is the will of the Father, that you believe on Him whom he has sent." Or it could be stated thus, "This is the will of the Father, that you believe on the Light of Christ that has been given to abide within you." This Christ Light is given to abide within you even as the life germ of the chick is given to abide in the egg. And as the evolving chick feeds on the yolk of the egg so is man's supply fully established.

As one learns to believe in that Christ Light, he will learn to feel Its divine reality and know of Its infinite power and experience its expanding glory. As he learns to become still he will learn to abide in It. He will also develop the ears with which to hear and the eyes with which to see. In that development he will learn to see the wonders of

eternity and hear the voice of the Almighty. As the Light
of Christ is thus contacted in the silent depths of one's soul,
Its powers become more and more operative in one's everyday life. One's messes are straightened out. One's weaknesses
are overcome. One's vision is expanded until he is able
"to overcome the evils of his life and loses every desire
for sin, and like the ancients, arrives at the point of faith
where he is wrapped in the power and glory of His Maker
and is caught up to dwell with Him."

It is in the inner stillness that one makes that divine contact with the redemptive Light of Christ and reaches the
point of development where he can actually KNOW GOD!

It is in this stage of progress that one leaves the apron
strings of his mother—earth—and steps out into the greater
world of his Father—the Spiritual world.

As one enters that inner stillness, or the "holy of holies",
within himself he will contact the very source of love. It
will fill his heart and soul and mind. Then with all his
strength he must use his energy to send that love forth
from the great heart center of his own being and from
every cell of his body and with every thought of his mind.
As he does this, he discovers that love arising as a living
flame from the very center of his soul. When this pure
devotion is accomplished, one reaches the point where that
glorified Light of Christ not only is comprehended but becomes *known*. It is where one finally *knows* Christ, for He
is the living source of that Light. As one holds his attention upon that Light he learns that Christ's redemptive
powers are contained in it. He also comprehends that Christ
Light is the holy altar flame within the temple of himself.
He knows fully that within the Light of Christ, the holy

flame of His Spirit, is contained all the powers of his own individual redemption.

As one learns to contact that Christ Light each day through a few selected periods, he will be taking time out to withdraw from the world of mother earth. In so doing he automatically enters into the world of his Father—even the world of higher powers and fuller manifestation. "Be Still" according to the things of the flesh and let the things of God begin to become apparent. "Be Still" and partake of the hidden manna of that divine Light of Christ, which "Bread of Life" is so necessary for one's spiritual development. It is only as one continues to partake of the divine spiritual food daily he can possibly grow into the Fullness of the Father.

As one continues in this practice of becoming still, at least as often as he takes time out for his mortal meals, he will not only learn of the source of his all-supply but will grow into another phase of existence. He will become aware of the great spiritual hunger after righteousness and as he learns to appease that hunger he will learn to KNOW God. As one continues to receive the divine, hidden manna of the "Bread of Life" in those periods of inner stillness, he naturally "grows in strength and waxes strong in spirit."

As one continues to partake of the spiritual food, or Christ Light, he learns of Its redemptive powers. He realizes that he is being cleansed and purified, "even as He is pure". This great Christ Light contains the power to right his errors and mistakes and to utterly consume his sins and weaknesses, for His Light is the flame of that holy, redeeming Light of Jesus Christ, the Lord and Redeemer of the world.

As one becomes thus cleansed and purified, that Christ

Light begins to expand and grow within the individual until it finally fills his entire being. When this is accomplished, the individual is prepared to open that great Christ door—even the door into eternal life—the door into another dimension—the front door into heaven—the door beyond death.

But no man can fulfill these higher things unless he *believes*—and is willing. He has to be willing to fulfill the higher laws by growing into them—even as the chick must grow into the full size of the egg. He must believe in the higher laws of righteousness, not self-righteousness, and begin to live them in love.

As that Christ door is opened the mortal veil or shell is completely rent. It is rent from top to bottom and one steps through into another phase of divine, glorified existence, for when that veil is rent nothing is impossible!

"But we know that, when he shall appear, we shall be like him; for we shall see him as he is. And every man that hath this hope purifieth himself, even as He is pure."

This is an individual accomplishment and must be brought about by each individual's own efforts. The purification is accomplished by one's learning to turn within in complete silence and contacting that Light of Christ, which holds the purifying powers of redemption in it. As one learns to open that inner, Christ door, he will become purified "even as He is pure". The learning to turn within in love and adoration is in itself a purifying glory. When one learns to hold himself constantly and consciously in that Christ Light, he is prepared for service.

These are the eternal, everlasting promises of God to the world and they have been waiting down the centuries for man to open his ears to hear. These promises are the

"Voice of Christ, which if a man hear and open that door, Christ will appear to him and feast with him." These promises are the eternal "Voice of Christ crying in the wilderness"—crying to be heard of man. "And any who hear that voice and open that door" will not only feast with the Redeemer of the world, but will also KNOW him. That inner hunger, that yearning of the Spirit, is Christ's knocking. But His voice is the crying of the promises for fulfillment. "Behold, I stand at the door, and knock: if any man hear my voice and open the door, I will come in and feast with him, and he with me." And that feasting will be on the very "bread of Life" and the individual who partakes thereof will never die.

These are the holy promises proclaimed by His Voice and are crying to be heard of man. If man will only open that door of his own soul they will all be fulfilled—and more.

The will of God for you is this: Learn to abide in that Christ Light within that He can begin to perform His Works through you. His works are miracles—not miracles to be seen of men—but miracles to bless and heal a world in silent love and eternal compassion.

"Wherefore, my beloved brethren, have miracles ceased because Christ hath ascended into heaven and hath sat down on the right hand of God, to claim of the Father his rights of mercy which he hath upon the children of men?

"And because he hath done this, my beloved brethren, have miracles ceased? Behold, I say unto you, Nay; neither have angels ceased to minister unto the children of men.

"For behold, they are subject unto him, to minister according to the word of his command, showing themselves unto them of strong faith and a firm mind in every form of godliness.

"Or have angels ceased to appear unto the children of men? Or has he withheld the power of the Holy Ghost from them? Or will he, so long as time shall last, or the earth shall stand, or there shall be one man upon the face thereof to be saved? Behold, I say unto you, Nay; for it is by FAITH that miracles are wrought; and it is by FAITH that angels appear and minister unto you; *Wherefore, if these things have ceased woe be unto the children of men, for it is because of unbelief, and all is vain.*"

In that contact with the Light of Christ, in the very center of your soul, is where the Will of God begins to operate and His perfection and His power begin to be released through you. He begins to do His works—of glory. Learn to abide in that center consciously and you will soon KNOW God.

THE OBEDIENCE LEARNED THROUGH SUFFERING

Chapter XIII

"Even I learned obedience by the things which I suffered," declared Christ humbly. Or, as it is recorded in Hebrews, Chapter five, verses eight and nine: "Though he were a Son, yet learned he obedience by the things which he suffered. And being made perfect, he became the author of eternal salvation unto all them that obey him." And then, as Christ so lovingly said, "When one has learned obedience there is no more need for suffering."

Christ's last test of obedience was passed in the Garden of Gethsemane, when in final and complete surrender he yielded his will to the will of God, the Father.

This obedience spoken of is not a blind, stupid obedience of deadened, indifferent relinquishing of one's powers. It is not the surrender or obedience of defeat. It is the triumphant obedience of overcoming. It is victory and glory, the point attained in which one becomes endowed with ineffable power. It is the utter, almost overwhelming, magnificence of comprehending the divine perfection and the unutterable glory of the Will of God.

This divine vision is attained only by lifting one's eyes to behold the glory of God and then by holding to that vision of exquisite, beautiful perfection.

As one's eyes become single to the glory of God he begins to comprehend the glory of God's infinite plan in creating the world. He begins to comprehend the great love

181

expressed in the creation of each and every child of earth, for each and every child is, first of all, a child of God.

In God's great love all are included. There were no favorites at the dawn of creation. There were not a few created above the others, nor were some created only to grovel and wallow in failure and despair. These conditions of failures and darkness have been of man's creating and of man's choosing because man has been blinded by the great ignorance.

In God's plan and in His Will only are the great perfection, the divine, triumphant glory, the supreme, healing love. And in that love and triumphant, sublime perfection are contained the eternal free-agency of man. Every man must make his own choice. He must develop and use his own will. He must make his own selections. He must learn the power of his own thinking and his own desiring. He must learn the suffering that is caused when he sets himself up contrary to the laws of progress, love, happiness and eternal goodness.

"Know ye not, that to whom ye yield yourselves servants to obey, his servant ye are to whom ye obey; whether of sin unto death, or of obedience unto righteousness." (Rom. 6:16).

When man has learned obedience by that which he suffers through his pride, his arrogance and his evils and follies, he learns that he is indeed a prodigal son who finds himself cast out and lonely, a wanderer in a strange land. Humbled and repentant, he becomes aware of a burning desire to return to his Father's house, if only as one of the least of his servants.

In that moment one realizes he has only messed up his life. In acquiring wealth he has forfeited the greater treasures of the soul. In seeking illicit loves he has become disgustingly satiated by his defiling indulgences. And in using his energies for selfish ends he has reached the downward track of life, empty of the great happiness he so eagerly anticipated. Every stolen joy only left its mark of deterioration and its decadent repulsiveness. His every wayward step only led him farther away from the happiness he expected to gather in huge quantities. His great pride turned into deep humiliation as his life crumbled into defeat. He may still be propped up by the soulless dollars he clutches in his hands, but their power to bring him pleasures and enjoyments has long since been dissipated. Or he may be left empty and penniless in some pensioners' lonely, forgotten retreat.

No matter what earthly road one may select to travel, there is always a certain amount of suffering connected with it until he learns the great obedience. No one can possibly escape the suffering of the road he travels in his willful ignorance. If one never looks beyond the cause to learn what created the suffering, if he never lifts his eyes to behold the glory of God, he will of necessity be stricken down eventually. There will come old age, sickness or senile feebleness. And all who travel the road of "self" will be claimed by death for death is the road mankind is traveling.

In his suffering and old age one may not be entirely forsaken. He may be permitted to spend his last, lingering days with his children—and be unwanted. He may live those last years entirely alone—and forgotten. Or, he may be in one of the most comfortable hospital beds in the world (and none of them are comfortable), or he may just drop dead without any long, lingering illness to prepare him in any way for death. But regardless of how he goes death will pry his fingers loose from all that he has so ardently clutched in his grasp, for in that last moment he will be stripped of all his life's gatherings, his authorities, his powers and his worldly possessions. Empty, as naked and alone as he came into the world, he will be taken through that back door, to be salvaged if he has not sinned too greatly.

Any individual traveling one of the mortal, selected roads of earth will suffer—and will die. Suffering, setbacks, disappointments and sorrows will dog his footsteps all the days of his life. And regardless of what his earthly gains have been, or to what physical, mortal level of achievement he attained, he never touched upon the beauties of perfection in one single phase of his rather empty and often wasted life. He suffered. He will continue to suffer until he learns of the great obedience that will not only free him, but glorify him.

Each individual lays claim to mortality just as much as mortality lays claim to the individual. It is a mutual embracing of complete willingness. Each man holds fondly to the things of earth. And the more violently wicked a man is the more desperately he struggles to cling to his soiled, frayed little thread of life.

When one has endured any degree of suffering whatsoever and *uses that suffering as a means to gain true knowledge,* he is taking a step into another realm of existence.

To escape the ills of life one does not need to commit suicide. That is not the way out. That is only the way into deeper suffering, more intense anguish and greater difficulty. It is impossible for anyone to run away from himself and the conditions his own thoughts and feelings, hence his actions, have created. Evil conditions can only be dissolved and transmuted into glory and light and power by one's learning to live in contact with that redeeming, purifying, glorifying Light of Christ, which is given to abide in every man who cometh into the world.

Christ gave the map to the road of overcoming, for even "He learned obedience by the things which He suffered." And when the obedience was learned the suffering ended.

All suffering is contained right within the personal will of man himself. Oh, he does not will the suffering. He only uses his will and his desires and his determination to follow his own way, and in so doing he creates the conditions which bring forth the suffering. He is a prodigal son gone out on his own, to follow the law of his own leading.

Accepting the creeds and doctrine of some church does not release one from the suffering. A church may help to turn one's mind to God, but usually the church wins out above God and one becomes completely sidetracked in his passive obedience to the church's conformity, or to its leaders. When one becomes impeded in his search for good through an organization, he will remain on the level of all physical, mortal suffering as that whirling vortex of evils holds him in its whims.

Only if one is courageous enough to lift his eyes to God and to Him alone, until his eyes become "Single to the very glory of God", can the pattern of evil and ills be broken. Sin and its cause will be completely left behind as one's eyes become single to the glory of God. And in that divine vision a new phase of existence is commenced.

At this stage one usually looks back upon his failures, his sufferings, his errors and mistakes, his sins and his weaknesses and realizing he can no longer carry the burden of them, he turns at last to God.

No mortal man has ever lived on this earth who has not sinned. "He who says he is without sin is a liar, and the truth is not in him." But sin, which has been caused by the great ignorance, can be overcome. It is overcome by banishing the ignorance which caused it. It is overcome in the search a man is invited to make—for God. It is overcome in the "asking, the seeking and the knocking" which God requires of all who would attain. It is overcome in the love that is developed through following the higher admonitions of the Almighty.

The sin, the suffering, the darkness and all evils have been caused primarily by the great ignorance. It has been man's great ignorance which has caused him to reject that divine Light of Christ, given to abide right within himself. In that Light is contained all the healing powers, the joy, the happiness and the glory of redemption, of complete forgiveness and eternal restoration.

As one accepts that divine Christ Light and no longer permits it to remain a rejected factor in his life, his life will take on new meaning. He will begin to be prepared for admittance into another realm, where all suffering, all lack and sorrow and evil are left forever behind.

In the purifying flame of that divine Christ Light the individual will become cleansed and purified from all sin. The sins, the weaknesses, the errors and mistakes will be consumed in that altar fire of Christ's holy Light.

As one's vision is lifted by this exalting experience his eyes truly become single to the glory of God. And in that revealing glory he beholds the breathtaking wonder of God's holy Will. He beholds the perfection contained therein. He comprehends for the first time the eternal, everlasting beauty of God's divine, holy plan. He sees and comprehends the love of God and views the wonders of His powers of unutterable, magnificent fulfillment, which has been dedicated and held in waiting for every child *willing* to accept the ineffable glory and wonder of such exquisite, manifested power.

Humble and love-filled, such an individual kneels at His throne in an obedience of grateful, utter surrender, yielding his own strident, rebellious, hateful will to the Will of God in a complete relinquishing. In this superb surrender he is prepared to take on immortality. He becomes one with God, or one with the Will of God. From henceforth he desires only the Will of God to be done, in which there is no suffering, no evil, no darkness, no sin or distress. The Will of God contains only that which is perfect. It contains the great, boundless glory of all that is good and beautiful enfolded in Its eternal light and filled with eternal love.

This is the point where one becomes *willing* to let God's Will be done. At this point one literally blends his own will with the Will of God. This is done without effort and completely without strife. It is accomplished by beholding a glimpse of just what His holy Will contains. As the individual comprehends all he has been fighting against as he has sought to live his own life unaided and in suffering and beholds that there is no need for the suffering; when he ceases "kicking against the pricks", his own will melts and dissolves in a love of adoring surrender that is exquisite in its beauty and the happiness it brings. This is how one actually becomes one with God. At this stage the individual reaches the point Christ achieved when He stated humbly and simply, "The Father and I are One."

When one has reached this state of attainment all seals will be removed. His whole being will be opened wide to the great Light and the perfect, divine love. The self will be conquered, overcome, outgrown and left behind. One becomes a holy chalice of glory held open for the Will of God to fill—even with the very "Fullness of the Father"— which IS the Fullness of His Will. This is also when one receives a "Fullness of Joy!" as promised to all those who attain. It is also the fulfillment of power and dominion and eternal glory.

One does not give up anything of value when he gives up his will. In releasing his will thus he gains all that is possible to receive. Then he discovers that he has not released his will at all. He has learned that he has only purified and perfected and glorified his own individual will to the extent that it can blend perfectly with the holy, divine Will of God. Man's will is thus exalted to the height and glory of God's perfect, holy Will. In this yielding and exalting process man becomes completely free. He is more free than he ever realized was possible. He is no longer bound by the shackles of earth. He comprehends the great TRUTH and becomes free indeed.

One reaches this divine point of exaltation and glory by first learning to accept all things that come to him as though they were direct from God and were sent as special privileges to him for his own training and purification. Just by being thankful in all things causes the higher laws of transmutation to begin to operate. Blessings begin to increase and to multiply and one begins to comprehend the joy and the glory of having all things added unto him. "He who is thankful in all things shall be made glorious;

and the things of this earth shall be added unto him a hundredfold; yea, more."

He who complains, continually finds fault or feels sorry for himself, shuts off the supply of his own blessings and the glory of God's great abundance. Only in gratitude can the law of increase be released and its powers of glorification become active.

There is nothing lacking in the Will of God for man's complete glorification, his eternal, exquisite enjoyment, his everlasting exaltation and his ultimate good *now*—and forevermore.

If you are depressed, if you lack, if you are suffering, if your messes have so involved you that you can see no possible way out, know that none of these conditions are the Will of God. It is never the Will of God that man should suffer. And all that is necessary to overcome the suffering is to learn the divine obedience that will blend your will with His Holy Will. Align yourself with His Holy Will and watch all adverse conditions transmuted into power and glory and ineffable joy.

In God's will is all-power and all-joy and all-happiness and all-good for you, with blessings so far beyond your present comprehension they have never even entered into either your mind or your heart. Yea, all that the Father has is yours and He is much more eager and anxious to bestow it upon you than you are to receive it. In His Will is only the great glory—even the glory which is your own, as you accept it—and are *willing*.

In this complete relinquishment of one's will, or rather, in the purified exaltation of one's will, is held the time when God will reveal Himself to the individual. This is the time for the complete fulfilling of all promises. This is the time of the complete purification. It is the time when one can behold the face of God. "For he will unveil His face unto you. It will be in His own time; and in His own way; and according to His own Will!" And in this greatest of all blessings and revelations one is bound to silence by the very unutterable glory and sacredness of knowledge so breathtakingly divine. "He who knows not God always tells it. He who knows God tells it not!"

The great obedience is the point of complete humility. It is the point where pride is destroyed, arrogance melted, love perfected. It is the point where the little mortal "self" is overcome or transformed in an obedience of reverent devotion that fulfills all perfection and reveals and bestows all power. It is the point where one actually KNOWS God.

THE LAST VEIL

Chapter XIV

There is one very simple way to fulfill all laws without strife or error or difficulty or even extreme striving. It is magnificently beautiful and perfect in its completeness as it leads one to that last, final veil and then gently removes that veil to reveal the face of God. That one most perfect entrance into the presence of the Father has been held forth from time immemorial.

The two great laws have been mentioned in the books preceding this one, but with this record has come the *time* of the complete unveiling of that first and great commandment and the divine power of its hidden secrets. Within that first holy law is contained the keys of eternity and the fullness of all things.

Christ only reiterated that most perfect, divine, holy law when He spoke these dynamic words: "Thou shalt love the Lord thy God with all thy heart, with all thy soul, with all thy mind and with all thy strength." Then He completed it by saying, "And thou shalt love thy neighbour as thyself." One could not possibly fulfill the first commandment without the second one being fulfilled also.

In the third book of the Bible, Moses reaffirmed the latter part of the law, which had existed from the very beginning, in the exact words Christ used centuries later: "Thou shalt love thy neighbour as thyself." (Lev. 19:18 and also verse 34).

In the book of Deuteronomy, that first and great commandment was recorded seven times in almost the exact
wording Christ used almost two millenniums later. (Deut.
6:5; 10:12; 11:1, 13, 22; 19:9; 30:6).

When Christ uttered the two great commandments that
would fulfill all others and all laws, He was not revealing
a new commandment. Neither was Moses proclaiming those
laws for the first time when they were recorded and placed
in his writings. Those commandments were established before the earth ever swung forth in its rhythmed harmony
within its destined orbit. Those eternal laws of glory hold
the keys of all progress, all perfection and all power. They
contain the very keys of eternity. They were revealed to man
when first he made his appearance upon this new-formed
earth.

Those laws of love were so far beyond and above the old
laws of Moses that few, preceding Christ's advent, paid
the least attention to them. Even the ancient Mosaic law
was difficult for many of earth's inhabitants in those days,
before the Christ. Then came the Redeemer of the world
with the higher law. Now mankind has advanced into the
living of the old Mosaic law, though they realize it not.
Those who most ardently profess to be Christians are but
living by that inferior, lesser law.

Only very recently have there been a comparative few who
are stepping beyond the multitudes and the ancient, inferior laws into the Way Christ revealed.

But it is now *time* to pass beyond the laws of unprogressiveness and retaliation and vengeance of "An eye for an
eye, and a tooth for a tooth." It seems almost ridiculous
to have to point out here that the law of retaliation is so
very apparent in almost all lives it has been almost entirely

unnoticed in its general acceptance. Sometimes it is even a more retrogressive law than the Mosaic one of ancient times. It is the habit or modern necessity to retaliate with something just a little more hurtful, a little more cutting, a little more violent than that which one received from another, even an acclaimed friend.

The greater laws have been almost as unheeded since Christ reaffirmed them as they were uncomprehended before His day.

It is *time* that the first and great commandment be comprehended and LIVED. Only in the *living* of it can the doors of eternity be opened.

Each separate part of the great commandment contains a definite key. The final key opens the door to the very presence of God, to the unveiling of His face.

These powerful keys I am commanded to place in your hands—for the *time* for their revealment is *now*.

These sacred keys I now place at your disposal as I lead you to the doors they unlock. It is up to you to use those keys and to turn those locks. If it were possible for me to open those doors, which it is not, you would never have the power to enter through those portals into the higher realms.

"Love God with all your heart," contains the first key. And now I will explain its power. "The heart", as stated in the book *To God the Glory*, does not mean the heart organ, but the great, living heart center. Within every man is the divine, spiritual heart-center that is like the center of a tree. When one loves with all his heart or innermost being, that great heart-center opens. It is the opening of this center which permits the Light of Christ to come forth. Or, it may be stated thus: within that divine center His

Light is contacted. That Christ Light contains the power to purify, to cleanse and to erase all sins and weaknesses. It has the power to eradicate the errors and mistakes, for within that Light is the power of each man's individual redemption. In the sacred flame of that Light one can be completely cleansed and purified as he begins to open his heart to Its divine reality and power. Within that Christ Light is also the power to know all truth and to contact all knowledge.

Love God with all your heart and you will release that divine Christ Light into your life in all Its fullness and Its ineffable power.

"Love God with all your soul." This is not to be just a pleasing phrase to the ears and then to be passed over. It means to literally extend that love of Christ, centered and contacted through the heart-center, into one's entire being. This divine love must be practiced daily, hourly and at all times. It must be LIVED with all the energy of one's soul. Contained within that love for God, which must be expressed through the soul of man, is the almost incomprehensible power of quickening and of renewal. It must be here understood that the soul includes every cell and atom, tissue and fiber of both the physical and spiritual man.

After one contacts that Christ love and His Light through opening his own heart-center, it becomes an easy thing to send that love out through his soul in ever increasing strength as he continues to practice it. As His love and Light thus flow out through the cells of the body, in unrestricted glory, it becomes vibrant and alive. This divine law of renewal is perfect and unfailing. It contains the powers of perfect healing and the vibrant life of eternal youth. "—for it is given to abide in you, that which quickeneth all things, and maketh alive all things." But no man can know the truth of this until he LIVES the law.

"Love God with all your mind." As one turns his mind continually toward God in a reverent devotion of pure love, he develops into the habit and power of divine thinking. He begins to think as God thinks, without condemnation, without stress, without discords, fears, hates or error. He thinks only the most beautiful things possible. Of necessity, he must love his neighbor as he loves himself. His mind will have developed into the power of thinking truly, purely, lovingly and uncondemningly. His every thought will become a seed of promise which plants its own rewards and its own glories. His thoughts will truly be allied with power as he reaches the point where he begins to comprehend all things—even God. One who thinks purely will have control over his life and the conditions surrounding him, for he will have become the master instead of the puppet of circumstances.

"Love God with all your strength." This is the crowning achievement and holds the final key. To love God with all one's strength unites the love of the heart, the soul and the mind into one current of definite, directed power. It gathers into one the powers of the heart, the soul and the mind in such a dynamic current of glory and light nothing can withstand it, on earth or in heaven. It is in the releasing of this stupendous current of love that the "self" is overcome. It is melted, or released without stress or striving. In this great love there is no need to battle or to strain.

When one's strength is energized to send forth the great love from the heart, soul and mind it releases the Light of Christ into the entire being of man. This released love conquers, subdues and glorifies the individual who will only practice it diligently until it becomes a part of his very life. Then only does one fully comprehend that he *is* actually *living* the law and is able to receive the fullness of its power. One grows into this great law by practicing and *living* it, not just by believing it. "Even the Devils believe, and tremble." But only those who live the laws or use the divine keys herein revealed can possibly *know* of their power.

As one loves God with all his strength he ceases wasting his energies on outside living. He reaches the point where his love is so concentrated, so perfect and so pure he begins to comprehend fully the great glory and power and perfection of God's holy Will. It is then his own little personal, mortal, selfish, erring will becomes so purified and exalted it blends with the Will of God in one magnificent harmony of united glory. In that divine blending the "self" is overcome and the individual is prepared to become one with God. Then it is that the last veil concealing the face of God can be removed.

When any individual reaches the point where love is fulfilled and made perfect and his will is completely purified and exalted to the very Will of God, then is God glorified in that individual.

It is in complete purification that God unveils His face to the individual. "It will be in His own time, and in His own way, and according to His own will." In other words, it will be when the individual is completely prepared and ready. And in that purified preparedness is the most natural experience, for one has grown into it.

This great and holy commandment of love most assuredly fulfills all laws and all righteousness.

Take the greatest of all commandments into your heart. Hold it in your mind. Practice it until it not only becomes a part of you, but you actually become it. Then only can you know of its ineffable power and its divine reality. Live it and you will soon KNOW God—and this is life eternal.

In the fulfilling of the great love one's life becomes dedicated to the higher ways of thinking and feeling—and being. As all one's strength is exerted in extending this love from the three main centers of his being, he enters into a higher, more sacred way of life and all his energies become concentrated in a love that includes and fills his entire being. He is no longer at war with himself. His being becomes attuned to peace and he is filled with Light. As he continues diligently to practice the great melody of love he becomes it. This practicing of love must be pursued faithfully and with all one's strength. It must be as desired a goal to reach the releasing of the divine symphony of love as it is to become a great and accomplished musician. Each requires diligent practice.

This love, when fulfilled, dissolves all pride, all arrogance and all evil. It clothes one in a tender, divine humility. It releases fully that song of inner praise and loving gratitude. It fills one with the divine Light of Christ until he does not have room to receive It—and so It flows out from him to multiply and increase his blessings and then goes on out to help redeem a world.

There is no fanaticism in this law of love. There could not possibly be. As one lives it he is no longer creed bound, nor will he worship amiss, nor have any other Gods before him. He will not permit some organization or church to sap the powers of his love and devotion, his strength and his soul and the energies of his mind while his heart remains empty, cold and unopened.

In the fulfilling of this commandment is "The Law of

the Lord" and the power of the Almighty as it is released in all its glory into the life of man.

In this great law is hidden the face of God. "Seek Him diligently, and you will find Him," . . . . . "For he will unveil His face unto you." . . . . "And this is life eternal, to know Thee, the only true and living God, and Jesus Christ, whom you have sent."

Practice this love constantly and find the temple of your own divine soul open wide to the very glory of God and to the ultimate revelation of Him Who waits anxiously on the other side of that final veil for you to reach through.

Practice this love and feel your soul grow into the perfection of His Fullness.

Practice this love and know that you are walking the sacred highway of God and will soon be prepared to be received into His embrace as eternity opens wide her great front doors to reveal to you her wonders.

Spend every spare moment of your life in sending out this love. Awake early and let your first thoughts be an inner song of love released to God. Go to sleep at night sending out this love to Him. Work as diligently on it as you work in serving the material world and you will soon be called to a service in that higher realm of Glory where all else is added.

This inward purifying and developing is the search for His kingdom—and His love is the righteousness that fulfills all laws.

The great love overcomes all things and fulfills all laws simply by the power of its eliminating all the adverse conditions of mortality.

The very instant one lets go of his misfortunes and calamities mentally and begins to adore and to glorify God in spite of all adverse conditions, or even for those conditions and is *willing* to accept them as the Will of God, in that instant those conditions will begin to be transmuted into blessings. This is the power of love. It is the reality of the first and great commandment in released action. One instantly begins to put on strength and power and by that very strength and power he becomes glorious. He leaves the neurotic, self-pitying realms of darkness, suffering and error behind and becomes clothed in Light and in majesty. At first that Light will be only a "feeling" or a singing vibration which grows as he learns to walk with God in a higher state of awareness. As he continues, he will realize that he is actually, literally clothed in Light and will soon grow into the very "Fullness of God". He will behold His face—and henceforth will actually KNOW God.

WOULDST THOU KNOW GOD?

Chapter XV

God will reveal His face to any who become completely purified and cleansed from all sin. In this greatest of all revelations possible to vouchsafe to men, the removal of the final veil will have to be accomplished through the individual's inner righteousness. The final, last veil is the one which conceals the face of God. When each individual is prepared through that inner purification and unfolding to receive this unspeakable blessing, so definitely promised by all the great and holy prophets from the beginning of time, God will fulfill His part. He will reveal Himself to the individual who has sought Him diligently. "If ye do as I say, then am I bound." This great, final revelation of unspeakable glory will be fulfilled when the individual has been tested and tried in all things and has been completely proved. It will be when he has proved his devotion and his love by his willingness to serve God at all hazards.

"For this is life eternal to know thee, the only true and living God and Jesus Christ, whom you have sent."

The full expressing and the living of the great, all-inclusive law of love, which automatically fulfills all other laws and all righteousness, has prepared the individual to receive all the promises. These promises include every promise ever given by God through His prophets, through His Beloved Son, Jesus Christ, or by Himself in direct revelation to the individual. This power to receive individual revelation is given to every man.

"We consider that God has created man with a mind capable of instruction, and a faculty which may be enlarged in proportion to the heed and diligence given to the light communicated from heaven to the intellect; and that the nearer man approaches perfection the clearer are his views, and the Greater his enjoyments, till he has overcome the evils of his life and lost every desire for sin; and like the ancients, arrives at the point of faith where he is wrapped in the power and glory of his Maker and is caught up to dwell with him."

It is quite necessary for the individual to progress into the state where he can contact that divine Light of Christ, so he can be personally instructed. This individual, personal contact must be made and developed before one can reach the point where he can actually *know* God. The time is at hand when all men must be prepared to be taught of God or be left behind. "And the weak things of the world shall come forth and break down the mighty and strong ones, that man shall not counsel his fellow man, neither trust in the arm of flesh—(mortal teachers).

"But that *every man* might speak in the name of God the Lord, even the Savior of the world:

"That faith might also be increased in the earth;" (D. & C. Sec. 1). This promise is verified in the fifty-fourth chapter of Isaiah, verse thirteen. It is also given in John, chapter six, and forty-five. Then Paul makes this marvelous statement, proving that not only his instruction, but his divine ordination had come direct from God: "For I neither received it of man, neither was I taught it, by the revelation of Jesus Christ." (Gal. 1:12)

As the last, final step of righteousness, or the "right use" of love and the laws of God has been fulfilled, the last veil will be removed and God will not only be able to teach His chosen ones, which are always the ones who choose Him; He will unveil His face to them and henceforth they will KNOW Him.

As man purifies himself all the veils will gradually be removed from the very first one, unbelief, which causes the hardness of heart and the blindness of mind, to that final one of the complete revelation of God. Each overcoming will reveal a higher vision and make apparent more light as one grows, like Christ, from grace to grace, into the very "Fullness of God."

To digress for an instant, let it be here noted that the more wicked a man is the more he bears witness to the living reality of God, as he constantly and continually calls upon His holy name in blasphemous profanity. The more defiled a man is the more he testifies to the eternal reality of God, as he continually calls upon the Name of God in vain. For whosoever uses the name of God, except in love and in blessing, is using it in vain. The curses he places upon all things In His Holy Name he is but placing upon himself.

Those who are fanatical speak His Name in a different way. They speak it as though they alone had a special right and claim upon His holy favors and His divine approval. And in shutting out the rest of humanity they are but excluding themselves from the pure inflow of His Holy Spirit and His eternal love and power.

Those who KNOW God remain silent. The awe and the wonder of God fills their entire beings with a knowledge so divine, so sacred and so pure it is almost impossible to analyze it even to themselves. They need not go about crying it aloud. Their very beings and their works bear witness.

When the final veil is removed one learns, as Christ learned, that the Father is within. And when the individual knows this the Father and the individual are truly ONE. "Believest thou not that I am in the Father, and the Father in me? The words that I speak unto you I speak not of myself: but the Father that dwelleth in me, he doeth the works. Believe me that I am the Father, and the Father in me: or else believe me for the very works' sake." . . . . . "In that day ye shall know that I am in my Father, and ye in me, and I in you." In that day when you will have reached the state of complete purification, you will know fully that God abides in you—and that you abide in Him, otherwise you could not abound. (John 14:10-11, 20).

It is only in this final purification and this ineffable revelation of God that one can fulfill the great hope and the prayer of Christ wherein He asked that "all might become ONE with Him, even as He and the Father were one."

As one completely purifies himself and is prepared to have that final veil removed and to receive the very "Fullness of the Father", he learns that God is indeed Omnipresent, Omnipotent and Omniscient. He actually becomes filled with this knowledge and with this power. He knows that God abides in him. And it is then that he actually KNOWS God and is no longer separated from Him.

This is life eternal. This is power ineffable. This is glory unspeakable. And from henceforth the individual no longer needs to go through life batting his head against stone walls and muddling everything he undertakes to accomplish by his own blundering. Henceforth the Father doeth the works—and nothing is then impossible—or imperfect.

If you have a desire to know and the courage to face it, if you are willing to open up your heart, your soul, and your mind to let God reveal Himself, I promise that never again will you need to be taught by fallacious mortals as you trust in the arm of flesh. It takes stupendous courage to throw off the binding shackles of a lifetime. It is painful indeed to begin to tear away the seals of years. It is as painful and as all-engrossing as the struggle the chick must put forth to free itself from its shell that it might step forth into a new realm, free, unhampered and unencumbered.

There is only one way to KNOW God and that is to "Seek Him diligently". This diligence means: without ceasing, with continued effort and with great energy and persistence. To seek truly and without bias it is necessary that one seeks as He instructed, through LIVING His laws. Only as His laws are LIVED is it possible to have the seals removed so the mind can be opened to permit God to reveal Himself. Those seals on the mind and heart and soul are the veils which must be overcome by humble, individual prayer asking, seeking and searching. The first veil is always the veil of unbelief. When unbelief is overcome Faith can be established. And when Faith is established KNOWLEDGE can become an eternal reality. "And knowledge is power."

I am not seeking to reveal God to you. I am only seeking to help you to open your own glorious mind—to give you a glimpse of the road of overcoming and what is waiting at the end of that journey of perfection as you purify yourself and seek to be perfect, even as He is perfect. The great, glorious revelation which unveils the Face of God can only be accomplished by God Himself. It will be when the individual has prepared himself to receive it. I am only commanded to write these things that your mind might in a measure be prepared to comprehend Him so He will be able, when you are prepared, to unveil His face unto you.

"Verily, thus saith the Lord; It shall come to pass that every soul who forsaketh his sins and cometh unto me, and calleth on my name, and obeyeth my voice, and keepeth my commandments, shall see my face and KNOW that I am;

"And that I am the true light that lighteth every man that cometh into the world;

"And that I am in the Father, and the Father in me, and the Father and I are one—

"The Father because he gave me of his fullness, and the Son because I was in the world and made flesh my tabernacle, and dwelt among the sons of men.

"I was in the world and received of my father, and the works of him were plainly manifest.

"And John saw and bore record of the fullness of my glory, and the fullness of John's record is hereafter to be revealed.

"And he bore record, saying: 'I saw his glory, that he was in the beginning, before the world was:

" 'Therefore, in the beginning the Word was, for he was the Word, even the messenger of salvation.

" 'The light and the Redeemer of the world; the Spirit of Truth, who came into the world because the world was made by him, and in him was the life of men and the light of men.

" 'The worlds were made by him; men were made by him; all things were made by him, and through him; and OF him.

" 'And I, John, bear record that I beheld his glory, as the glory of the Only Begotten of the Father, full of grace and truth, even the Spirit of Truth, which came and dwelt in the flesh, and dwelt among us.

" 'And I, John, saw that he (Christ) received not the fullness at the first, but received grace for grace.' " (Or, for each grace developed and fulfilled he received another grace to add to his gradually increasing virtues and perfection.)

" 'And he received not the fullness at first, but continued from grace to grace until he received a fullness.

" *'And thus he was called the Son of God, because he received not of the fullness at the first.*

" 'And I, John bear record, and lo, the heavens were opened, and the Holy Ghost descended upon him in the form of a dove, and sat upon him, and there came a voice out of heaven saying: this is my beloved Son.

" 'And I, John bear record that he received a fullness of the glory of the Father.

" *'And he received all power, both in heaven and on earth, and the glory of the Father was with him, for he dwelt in him.'*

"And it shall come to pass, that if you are faithful you shall receive the fullness of the record of John.

"I (Jesus Christ) give you these sayings, THAT YOU MAY UNDERSTAND AND KNOW HOW TO WORSHIP, AND KNOW WHAT YE WORSHIP: THAT YE MAY COME UNTO THE FATHER IN MY NAME, AND IN DUE TIME RECEIVE OF HIS FULLNESS.

"FOR IF YE KEEP MY COMMANDMENTS YE SHALL RECEIVE OF HIS FULLNESS, AND BE GLORIFIED IN ME AS I AM IN THE FATHER.

"And now, verily I say unto you, I was in the beginning with the Father, and am the Firstborn.

"YE WERE ALSO IN THE BEGINNING WITH THE FATHER: THAT WHICH IS SPIRIT, EVEN THE SPIRIT OF TRUTH.

"THE SPIRIT OF TRUTH IS OF GOD. I AM THE SPIRIT OF TRUTH. And John bore record of me saying, He received a fullness of truth, yea, even of all truth.

"AND NO MAN RECEIVETH A FULLNESS UNLESS HE KEEPETH HIS COMMANDMENTS.

"He that keepeth his commandments receiveth truth and light, until he is glorified in truth and knoweth all things.

"MAN WAS ALSO IN THE BEGINNING WITH GOD. INTELLIGENCE, OR THE LIGHT OF TRUTH, WAS NOT CREATED OR MADE, NEITHER INDEED CAN BE."

The foregoing, great and unspeakable truths must begin to be comprehended by man in order that the final revelation of God might be given.

In the following scripture is revealed the same pattern and the same possibility for man as Christ accomplished through His divine achievement of overcoming the flesh: "He that is ordained of God and sent forth, the same is appointed to be the greatest, notwithstanding he is the least and the servant of all.

"WHEREFORE, HE IS POSSESSOR OF ALL THINGS: FOR ALL THINGS ARE SUBJECT UNTO HIM, BOTH IN HEAVEN AND ON EARTH, THE LIFE AND THE LIGHT, THE SPIRIT AND THE POWER SENT FORTH BY THE WILL OF THE FATHER THROUGH JESUS CHRIST HIS SON.

"BUT NO MAN IS POSSESSOR OF ALL THINGS

EXCEPT HE BE PURIFIED AND CLEANSED FROM
ALL SIN.

"And if ye are purified and cleansed from all sin, ye
shall ask whatsoever you will in the Name of Jesus and it
shall be done."

Man, on this earth, is the very least of all the advancing
Spirit children of God in regard to power and understanding, because his spiritual intelligence has been so clouded
with the mortal seals and veils of darkness caused by sin
and transgression. When man overcomes the desires of the
flesh the seals will drop away. Then will the blindness be
removed from his mind and the darkness from his heart
and his understanding will expand until he will be able to
comprehend all things—even God. Man will then be prepared to receive of His Fullness—and with that Fullness of
God he truly becomes the greatest, though he becomes the
most humble, the most selfless and the most self-effacing
as he seeks to glorify only God.

Would that I were permitted to reveal to you at this
time the complete meaning of the foregoing scripture. All
I am permitted to give is the following: "Therefore it is
given to abide in you: the record of heaven; the Comforter;
the peaceable things of immortal glory; the truth of all
things; that which knoweth all things, and hath all power,
according to wisdom, mercy, truth, justice and judgment."
Could the foregoing powers be anything less than the very
powers of God Himself? Analyze them. Ponder them in
your heart. And begin to lay claim to them.

I am permitted to point out another clue which leads to
the unveiling of the face of God: "And the Light which
shineth, which giveth you light, is through him who en-

lighteneth your eyes, which is the same light which quickeneth your understandings:

"Which light proceedeth forth from the presence of God
to fill the immensity of space—

"The light which is in all things, which giveth life to all
things, which is the law by which all things are governed,
*even the power of God, who sitteth upon his throne, who
is in the bosom of eternity, who is in the MIDST of all
things.*"

These are the promises and the powers that go beyond
all orthodox rituals and conformity. They have nothing
whatsoever to do with apparel or styles, beards or the
length or style of either one's dress or one's hair, or with
any outside emptiness. These great powers mentioned are
the powers of God. And these powers are a very part of
man, for "All that the Father has is yours". These powers
are centered in man. They are given to abide in him. They
are only awaiting man's awakening vision and his acceptance of them to become operative.

"The earth rolls upon her wings, and the sun giveth his
light by day and the moon giveth her light by night, and
the stars also give their light, as they roll upon their wings
in their glory, in the midst of the power of God.

"Unto what shall I liken these kingdoms, that ye may
understand?

"Behold, all these are kingdoms, and any man who hath
seen any of the least of these hath seen God moving in
his majesty and power.

"I say unto you, he hath seen HIM; Nevertheless, he who
came unto his own was not comprehended.

"The light shineth in darkness, the darkness comprehendeth it not; Nevertheless, the day shall come when *you*

shall comprehend even God, being quickened in him and by him.

"Then shall ye know that ye have seen me, that I am, and that I am the true light that is in you, and that you are in me, otherwise ye could not abound" (or exist).

"Inasmuch as you strip yourselves from jealousies and fears, and humble yourselves before me, for ye are not sufficiently humble, the veil shall be rent and you shall see me and know that I am—not with the carnal neither natural *mind,* but with the Spiritual (mind).

"For no man has seen God at any time in the flesh except quickened by the Spirit of God.

"Neither can any natural man abide the *presence* of God, neither after the carnal mind.

"Ye are not able to abide the presence of God now, neither the ministering of Angels, wherefore, continue in patience until you are perfected."

One becomes "quickened" by the process of purification and in fulfilling the great law of love. Only when this has been completely accomplished is one prepared to abide the presence of God or receive of His Fullness. The promise is that those who are purified shall receive of the very Fullness of God. Many receive only a degree of His Holy Spirit and are completely satisfied. No one should ever be satisfied with less than that promised FULLNESS.

"If ye abide in me, I will abide in you."

"If a man love me he will keep my words; and my Father will love him, and we will come into him and make our abode with him." (John 14:23).

"Behold, I stand at the door and knock; if any man hear my voice, and open the door, I will come into him—"

There are numerous passages of scripture which man

has completely ignored in his searching for partial truths. Man has only desired to find that which conforms to his own pre-conceived ideas or his orthodox beliefs.

If one is to comprehend God through the quickening of his being and comprehend Him with the Spiritual mind, man must become spiritualized through purification, which is not accomplished through outward forms but through a sanctification of his very life through *Living* the higher laws. He must be prepared, through a complete inner dedication and a divine love that rises above the little mortal "self" and all its past conformities.

"If no man has seen God at any time in the flesh, except quickened by the Spirit of God", then the flesh must be exalted and spiritualized by the power of God and lifted into a higher vibration of glory. In this higher, quickened vibration, which must also exalt the flesh to the status of the Spirit, one can be prepared to behold the face of God.

I started to write a very self-evident fact, but was forbidden. And so I shall only make this remark: God has stated, "This is my Beloved Son, in whom I am well pleased." Any individual who has learned to contact that Light of Christ, through the great quieting of his inner being, will begin to be filled with that Light. In that great inner stillness of man's own soul his being becomes quickened and lifed into a higher vibration of glory. In that individual, the Great I am, God, is indeed well pleased. And when that I am, God, who has been contacted through the great inner stillness, is well pleased through the sanctification of that individual's life, that individual becomes "His Beloved Son." . . . . . "This is my Beloved Son, in whom the I am, is well pleased."

This great revelation is not just something which happens to the individual. This could not possibly be. The laws must be fulfilled. The laws have been waiting forever and forever, even from the beginning, for man to *believe*, to *live* and to *fulfill*. When man is *willing,* or when his individual will is exalted and completely purified, *man* happens to *it.*

When the individual's will is purified and exalted to blend with the Divine Will they become as One, perfect, powerful and all-fulfilling.

When one has developed the power of being able to turn to God in every thought, the mind becomes purified and love-filled. It is then one begins to think as God thinks. It is then God's thoughts begin to express in glorious perfection through that purified mind of the individual. And God's thoughts are all-powerful, they are all-knowing, infinite and eternal. It is then one not only comprehends all things but actually knows all things and has all power. "All things become subject unto him, both in heaven and on earth; the light and the life; the Spirit and the Power." And one becomes the greatest. This is where mortality is left behind.

Chapter XVI

Immoral thoughts place vulgar expressions on the human face divine. And those thoughts begin their defiling process upon the whole being of man. Vulgar thoughts, vulgar stories, immoral emotions and most of all, immoral actions wash the entire body and countenance in a mud bath of filth. And that filth lingers. If such thoughts, emotions and actions become habitual their defilement begins to write its permanent record upon the whole physical being of man.

No man is immune from the results of encouraged evil. No one can escape the results of his thinking and feeling habits. They are the chiselling tools by which faces are molded and carved. The waves of thought vibrations set the pattern the face and body must assume as time goes on. It takes time to mold a human form. It has to grow into the pattern held out to it. And none can escape from the design they themselves select to mold themselves by. The results are as inevitable as the pattern of the night following the day.

Discords, hates, fears, self-pity, greed, dishonesty, any of the perversions, any ugliness of thought and feeling are the carvers of the being of man. A line is etched here, another there, as tissues and muscles begin to sag and crumble before the onslaught of the sculptor's tools. Each individual is his own sculptor, his own constructor, his own engraver. "Man is made or unmade by himself; in the armory of thought he forges the weapons by which he destroys himself; he also fashions the tools with which he builds for himself divine attributes and powers of joy and strength and peace. By the right choice and true application of thought, man ascends to the divine Perfection; by the abuse and wrong application of thought, he descends below the level of the beasts. Between these two extremes are all the grades of character, and man is his maker and master." (AS A MAN THINKETH—James Allen). Man is not only the carver of his future but of his face, his figure and his life.

One of the reasons husbands and wives begin to look alike after years of congenial association is because they are in tune to the extent they think the same kind of thoughts.

No matter how exquisitely beautiful a girl may be in her girlhood or how handsome a boy may be in his youth, they can become broken-down, ugly human beings by middle life—and very often are. Those who have nothing but a pretty face to offer a world will soon lose it unless their thoughts are as beautiful and lovely as their faces. And those who are homely and ugly can become attractive, even beautiful by the use of right thinking.

No matter how beautiful or how handsome, how perfectly formed an individual may be, how attractive and admired when youth still holds its throne, that individual will remold and remodel himself according to the thought patterns permitted to rule in his or her emotions.

There are those who have been very unattractive, even homely, in youth, who become good-looking in middle life. The face of youth is the face bequeathed through a heritage already ascribed to. But that bequest is only as temporary as the clean canvas awaiting the artist's brush, or the blank sheet awaiting the recordings of the scribe. A new, young face is but the plastic, unfinished handiwork of God, awaiting the course and decisions made by the individual himself. A new, young face is but a mass of soft, delicate clay awaiting the engraver's touch. Each individual is the engraver, the sculptor, the artist, the scribe and recorded as he carves and records his very thought. Some are only passing shadows and hence are speedily erased. Other thoughts become deep furrowed through habit and repetition.

Every thought and feeling that is out of harmony with the infinite song of the universe, the joy of love and praise and singing gratitude is sin. As sin begins to leave its mark the signs of age commence.

This is most easily observed in the faces of some movie stars. Their beauty is usually but a swift and passing dream— a memory. Their handsome faces become too soon a vanishing gift of fading loveliness. For only a few short years they carry the glorified promise of that which was meant to be—the promise of what was meant to have become permanent if only the higher laws had been fulfilled.

To be a great actor or actress, it is necessary to both think and feel each and every part. It is necessary to actually *live* them. Each part becomes real—and that reality is engraved upon the plastic structure of the actor, leaving its indelible mark. If the parts are difficult or evil the individual is the more speedily destroyed. The character actors who take hideous, cruel parts are all short-lived.

The last part Wallace Beery played upon the screen caused his death. It was too intense, too violent and required too much abnormal thinking and feeling to permit Wallace to remain immune to its destructive force. Wallace was a kindly, understanding man with a big heart and he could not long survive the violence of the last parts he portrayed. Every strident word, every cruel thought, every abhorrent deed, every strident emotion tore through his own being as he played the game of make believe too seriously. He lived his parts so completely and so convincingly he reaped the results of his own acting.

One of the most difficult and speedily degenerative professions is being a character actor when the parts one is called to play are cruel, ugly and vicious.

Yet the harm of pretending such parts is only secondary to actually *being* the type of individual who is lustful, greedy, avaricious, cruel, hate-filled, vengeful and completely immoral and wicked.

It is also very harmful for any individual, especially children, to behold a predominance of such plays—or parts. This is the reason why comic books, which usually aren't funny at all but violent, tragic, vengeful stories of crime and evil, must be outlawed. This is also why violent television programs and violent movies are so injurious and so detrimental.

Any portrayed violence that claims the attention of an individual will leave its mark upon his being. To children, these are not only watched but re-lived—even though it be in a second-hand way. And in the living, their wide-open minds drink in the vibrations which will begin to transform their very cells and tissues. Even in early childhood the sculptor is at work designing the form age will assume.

At the present day it is utterly impossible to shield an individual from all evil. To do so would not be wise and would accomplish no good at all. It would only make such an individual a "neutral", without his having been permitted to use his free-agency in making his own choice. Such an enforced condition is doubly harmful. Sooner or later one is going to be thrust out upon the battlefield of life to meet its issues, to be tested and tried. Those too shielded are the least prepared for the shock and reality of the battle of life. They are too easily conquered by the evil forces. But to be perfectly fit and prepared for the great testing does not require that one be hurled against extreme violence in infancy or early childhood.

One must meet life's issues in order to make decisions and use his free-agency. He must exert his power to choose in order to become strong and filled with understanding, wisdom and goodness.

Some erroneously believe that because Satan's evils and temptations are placed in man's path at every turn one should participate in every form of transgression in order to comprehend the great issues of life. This idea is not only false but extremely dangerous as well. Willful participation in evil removes all spiritual protection and leaves one completely exposed by his own folly. The idea of participating in transgression willingly, so one may know what it is all about, is one of the most deceptive impositions and insidious mockeries of Satan's destructive designs. And for those who accept his invitation to participate, even slightly, he has the power to glamorize his enticements and his defiling, broken laws.

The more one refrains from evil and temptation, both in thought and action, the stronger he will be and the less hold evil will have upon him.

There is no individual who lives upon this earth who will not have to face the enticings and temptations and the violent influence of darkness and evil until they are completely overcome by man's own progressive advancement. Children who have been too shielded and those who have relied on others to do their thinking for them develop no strength or power with which to resist evil when it is thrust upon them.

All children should be nurtured and cared for, but they should be taught to make their own decisions. Above all they should be TAUGHT TO LOVE. And all children should know the effects of hate and the power of love.

Children are taught vengeance and spite and retaliation almost from birth. The baby falls upon the floor and bumps itself and a doting loved one will hit the floor, saying, "Naughty old floor for hurting baby." That, of course, may not be the exact situation or phrasing, but it is the general idea and by it almost every child is taught the harmful trait of revenge, vengeance, against anything and everything that hurts or injures him or stands in his way.

When the human thoughts and emotions can be trained to love, to feel compassion and kindness and to live in happiness, to know joy, then faith will not be far behind.

When peace can be established within a human heart, when love becomes the predominating attribute, the surpassing virtue and when gratitude sings forth in every cell and fiber, then will age be retarded and disease overcome. When that love and praising gratitude become the living reality of one's life youth can be retained. When one's being becomes so imbued with love that it is all his heart or emotions feel, all his soul knows and all his mind ever thinks, the ravages of age and sin will begin to be erased and youth can be reclaimed.

The full wage of sin is death. The intermediate wages of sin are deterioration, wrinkles, old age, illness and ugliness of action, appearance and thought. All of which lead to that grim back door of death.

Every unkind thought leaves a muscle weakened. Every angry word leaves its definite scar. Every thought of fear, envy or hate carves its etchings on the human form divine. Greedy, vengeful, immoral, evil thoughts, thoughts of worry or pain go out through every cell and tissue of the body, marking their trails and constructing their inroads of decay for every other ill and ugliness to follow on their heels.

It is not only necessary to train children to refrain from discords, negatives and anger, but they must also be taught WHY. It is most necessary that all be instructed in the principles of love and joy and the great powers of happiness and peace and how the laws work. As love is harbored, or is, to be more exact, generated in the human heart then sent out through the soul by man's own thought processes, his physical body will not only be renewed but will maintain the gift of eternal youth.

No young person can ever visualize himself or herself changing or growing old any more than the average human being figures on dying. These conditions are not the living concepts which mankind naturally has embedded in its *instinctive* make-up. Why? Because both old age and death were never intended in the beginning. Both are conditions Lucifer has imposed upon man through his yielding himself to the negative forces and influences of evil.

The first and great commandment fulfills the higher law perfectly and in its entirety. When the heart is opened so the divine Christ-like love can be generated through it, the great power of renewal is placed in the hands of the individual. When that love is sent into every cell, fiber, tissue and nerve of man's being, regeneration commences. When one uses his mind to keep this love forever uppermost, as he reverently and lovingly sends his adoration to God, his mind will begin to be enlightened and his understanding expanded. Then, when the three great forces within man—heart, soul and mind—are united with all one's strength, there is released the quickening, spiritual power of divine renewal right from within man's own being. The more one becomes aware of the infinite, ineffable power of this quickening life force within, the more speedily can his own body and face take on the properties of his lost youth. The law is eternal and unfailing. It has been incomprehensible to man only because man has never believed in Christ enough to LIVE the law.

This love is much more than the love of a man for a maid or the love of a maid for a man. This great love for God, which must be perfected, is completely beyond sex or personalities, although those who have been shot by cupid's arrow are much more alive and vibrant than those who are untouched by even this inferior type of personal love. The divine love is all-inclusive. It is as vast as eternity. It cannot be expressed in declamation or in flowery phrases. It is a love as deep as the soul and more real than life itself. This love that is required must be pure and unfeigned. It must be compassionate, tender and undefiled. It must be as far-reaching as the creative love of God. It must become the exclusive *allness* of those who travel the road of Light and receive of its powers and its renewing, quickening, vibrating glory. The perfect love is the great ONENESS with God.

When any individual lifts his eyes to the higher vision, to the glory of God, his heart expands in exquisite strains of released love. Then, when his mind and strength unite in maintaining these glorious gifts and redevelops them, the evils of his life will be completely overcome. For in this way old age is banished and death conquered. "Oh grave where is thy victory? Oh death, where is thy sting?" These things are overcome in the love of "Christ's redeeming Light, which has been given to abide in every man who cometh into the world".

By such overcoming, sin and death and Satan will be bound and will lose all power. Suffering, old age, ugliness of form and feature, disease and death are the scars of Lucifer's regime. Even these scars can be healed if only one will leave the darkness and step forth into the great Christ Light, triumphant and free.

"I AM THE WAY!"

Chapter XVII

In Scripture God is called "the Father of Lights!" He is indeed the Father of all who bring forth the Light of Christ from within. When *that* Light is contacted and brought forth one becomes a *son*. "This is my beloved son, in whom I am well pleased," or in whom I AM, which is the Light of Christ, is well pleased.

The deep, eternal I Am within man is the glorified reality of "the Light of Christ that is given to abide in every man who cometh into the world". In this light is contained Christ's quickening, redeeming power of renewal and forgiveness. It is the seat of all-knowing that is given to abide right within man. It contains all peace and all power. "For it is given to abide in you; the record of heaven; the Comforter; the peaceable things of immortal glory; the truth of all things; that which quickeneth all things, which maketh alive all things; that which knoweth all things, and hath all power, according to wisdom, mercy, truth, justice and judgment."

"The Light of Christ is given to abide in every man who cometh into the world." The Light of Christ contains all the powers held within the first of these two quotations.

Within the Light of Christ is also contained the powers of complete purification and of redemption, the power that fulfills all promises and the power and intelligence which can straighten out all one's tangles and messes, his errors

222

and his mistakes. The Light of Christ contains and reveals all truth as Its dynamic, blue ray is brought forth and put into use.

The Light of Christ alone can give minute instruction in the affairs of life. It is not necessarily a light to just the physical eyes, though that is part of Its function. Its real purpose is spiritual and It gives Its greatest Light to the intellect of him who is open to receive and who has overcome the blindness of his mind through learning to believe.

As one follows the direction of His leading he will be led into *all truth,* for "The Christ Light IS THE WAY"! If a man follows that Light, or travels according to Its inner instructions he cannot possibly err, or fail. The Christ Light alone is the infallible guide to one's own individual journey of life—abundant and full. This is the Way Christ traveled. It is the Way which He IS. "For I Am the Way, the Truth and the Life!"

"Enter ye in at the strait gate: for wide is the gate, and broad is the way, that leadeth to destruction (or death), and many there be which go in thereat.

"Because strait is the gate, and narrow is the way, which leadeth unto life, and few there be that find it.

"Beware of false prophets, which come to you in sheep's clothing, but inwardly they are ravening wolves."

"The strait and narrow way" is not some orthodox belief, creed or ritual conformity, as so many have supposed. It is not any narrow doctrine expounded in blindness. "The strait and narrow way" is the inner path, revealed and made clear by the great Christ Light. It is the way of personal instruction and minute direction to each and every individual who will only give heed to it. It is the way known to the ancients as The Inner Way, or "The Inner Doctrine!"

The Christ Way is fulfilled in the admonition, "Do all that thou doest in the name of the Lord, and call upon the name of the Son forevermore."

"The strait and narrow Way" is the way of definite, individual, personal instruction in which one performs no act, speaks no word except that directed by the Light, that source of All-knowing Power. It is the path in which one learns to abide in Christ, in His Light, and that Light becomes more and more apparent to, and in, the individual.

That Light of Christ is truly "The bread of life, which, if a man partakes thereof he will never hunger nor thirst again".

Within the Light of Christ is the power of contact with all the great store of God's infinite abundance so one advances to the point where it is no longer necessary to labor for the things that perish, for all these things will be added unto him.

There are thousands who have advanced to the point where they contact, in a lesser degree, this holy Light, or Christ power. Then they begin to use it, as Christ Himself was tempted to use it, for bread, honor, self-aggrandizement. They begin to use His healing ray for money, for a price, or begin to preach for hire. All who thus MIS-use His holy Power for personal livelihood, for their own support or for honors, will never be able to advance into the "Fullness of the Father". Nor can they possibly go on to their "HIGHER" reward. Only he who labors for God is worthy of "his higher wage" and is entitled to sonhood. Every individual's progress is definitely stopped when he compromises and becomes willing to receive a menial's pay in earthly coin, worldly security. Those who accept money for any service, in the name of the Lord, are being deceived. As they receive their pay, or reward from the world the world becomes their paymaster. They do not realize they have forfeited the greater reward for that mediocre feeling of personal, physical security and well-being. They have sold themselves for hire to the world—and from the world they accept their pay, therefore they are serving the world—not God. "No man can serve two masters."

"Not everyone that saith unto me, Lord, Lord, shall enter into the kingdom of heaven; but he that doeth the will of my Father which is in heaven.

"Many will say to me in that day, Lord, Lord, have we not prophesied in thy name? And in thy name have cast out devils? And in thy name done many wonderful works?

"And then will I profess unto them, I never knew you: depart from me, ye that work iniquity."

"Iniquity" is any unjust or unlawful act that is out of harmony with the infinite laws of the Universe. It is an act that is contrary to the divine law of God to receive earthly compensation for services rendered in His Name. To charge any fee for rendering any service "In the Name of the Lord" is a transgression and an error.

Those who labor for Christ must render that service through love and *freely*. It must be without price. His gifts and powers are given to be used for the benefit of man and not for money. They must be rendered without earthly compensation. His divine gifts must be used even as Peter and John used them in healing the lame man at the temple gate. They looked upon him with infinite compassion and Peter proclaimed, "Silver and gold have I none; but such as I have *give* I to thee. In the name of Jesus Christ of Nazareth rise up and walk."

When the healing powers of Christ and any of the holy gifts of power are used to obtain money one is no longer laboring for Christ. He is working for his own living and for the pay of the world. Such will receive his reward from the world and in so doing the world is accepted as his paymaster and not God. Such an individual cannot possibly expect any credit, reward or acknowledgement from God or Christ. He has placed himself in the status of a menial and will receive a menial's pay—the wages of the world— even death.

Within the Light of Christ is contained the perfect Will of God. As one is directed by the holy Light of his own individual pattern, as contained in the Will of God, or in the perfect plan, the Will of God will be exalted and fulfilled in the individual. It is then that one can become sanctified. Those who comprehend and fulfill these laws are advanced into a rate of higher vibration. They become "worthy of their hire" (higher) enlightenment and exaltation.

No individual can perform any great work. Only as the Light of Christ is brought forth can anything of permanent value be accomplished. It is through the Light of Christ, which is given to abide within man, that "God doeth His works". It is within and through the Light of Christ that all things are made possible.

"—The Light of Truth. Which truth shineth. THIS IS THE LIGHT OF CHRIST. As also he is in the sun, and the light of the sun, and the power thereof by which it was made.

"As also he is in the moon, and is the light of the moon, and the power thereof by which it was made;

"As also the light of the stars, and the power thereof by which they were made;

"And the earth also, and the power thereof, even the earth upon which you stand.

"And the light shineth, which giveth you light, is through him who enlighteneth your eyes, which is the same light that quickeneth your understandings:

"WHICH LIGHT PROCEEDETH FORTH FROM THE PRESENCE OF GOD TO FILL THE IMMENSITY OF SPACE—

"The light which is in all things, which giveth life to all things, which is the law by which all things are governed, EVEN THE POWER OF GOD, *who sitteth upon his throne, who is in the bosom of eternity,* WHO IS IN THE MIDST (middle or center) OF ALL THINGS."

This is just about as enlarged a description of the Light of Christ as is possible to obtain on this earth. But as this Light of Christ is comprehended and brought forth from within the individual there is much more that must be revealed.

"For you shall live by every word that proceedeth forth from the mouth of God.

"For the WORD *of the Lord is truth, and whatsoever is truth is Light, and whatsoever is Light is Spirit;* EVEN THE SPIRIT OF JESUS CHRIST.

"And the Spirit giveth light to every man that cometh into the world; and the Spirit enlighteneth every man through the world, that harkeneth to the voice of the Spirit."

(And "those who rejecteth that Light of Christ, or who harkeneth not to Its Voice are under condemnation".)

"And everyone that harkeneth to the voice of the Spirit cometh unto God, even the Father.

"And the Father teacheth him of the covenant which he has renewed and confirmed unto you—"

"And the whole world lieth in sin, and groaneth under darkness, and under the bondage of sin.

"And by this you may know that they are under the bondage of sin, because they come not unto me.

"For whoso cometh not unto me is under the bondage of sin.

"And whoso receiveth not my voice is not acquainted with my voice, and is not of me." Or in other words, "They know not the God in Whom they can trust."

The voice of God is heard through that Light of Christ when one develops It and becomes in harmony with It. This divine voice is the voice of instruction and of revelation. It is the voice of inner joy and gladness. It is a song in the heart when one is in tune with the exalting, sanctifying, triumphant symphony of the Universe. The Christ Light is also the inexplicable voice and power of peace. It is the revealing expression of the Holy Spirit of Promise that comes as a breath, a whisper or the powerful revelation of complete knowledge when one opens his heart to hear—and his mind to comprehend. The voice of the great Christ Light is heard in every warm, joyous approval felt from within when one has performed some kind act, spoken a loving word or refrained from some evil deed. It is that Voice which is also heard in rebuke for every evil, selfish, violent thought or act.

It is as one learns to give heed to the deep, inner Voice of Christ's holy redeeming Light that he is definitely traveling the Way which leads to Life eternal.

This is the Way Christ traveled. It is the Way of His Light. It is the "strait and narrow Way" which leads to the great door of magnificent, eternal, exalted life. It is a personal Way designed for each individual to travel. It is as private as the inner life and feelings of one's own unsharable thoughts. It is not the way of the multitude, nor of the group, nor of organizations. It is so completely individual that of necessity each must travel it alone. Because it is so still and quiet and alone is the reason it has been so difficult to find.

This quiet inner way is not the broad, much traveled, open road of the masses. The multitudes and groups cannot travel it together for it is an individual, inner path. It is not the broad road of outward living. It is not a wide path of outside conformity, nor is it a path of outward rituals which cleanse only the outside of man. It is not the broad, open way followed by the throngs, as it leads to destruction and through which the many enter.

The inner Way Christ traveled is the road to Life Eternal. It is the road that by-passes death.

Only as one contacts that Light of Christ within and follows Its divine leading can he possibly receive the gifts and powers which are promised "TO ALL THOSE WHO BELIEVE—EVEN UNTO THE ENDS OF THE EARTH". One's *belief* must embrace that Light within and then hold to it with tenacious determination. He must follow Its leading in all things. And as one learns to follow, It will lead him to the Father. On such is the gift of Eternal life bestowed. It is then the great, last veil of Light dissolves and the face of God, the Father, is revealed. It is then that one is privileged to actually KNOW God.

This is the knowledge which is power. This is His Kingdom—the Kingdom of Heaven within. Those who are privileged and worthy to enter this kingdom become members of the Church of the First Born, even of Jesus Christ, the Lord.

This is a sacred, individual road and must be traveled from within. None can travel it who remain upon the broad, outside path of the multitudes and who conform to the mass acceptance of rituals and orthodox behavior and forms. This Way is the HIGHER Path that permits one to fulfill his own individual pattern of transforming perfection as he learns to step into Spiritual maturity and Walks henceforth with God—his Father.

This holy Path of Light is entered by fulfilling that first and greatest of all commandments, not just in theory but by literal adherence and constant practice.

As one loves God with a devotion that is beyond words, as it vibrates forth in inner praise and gratitude, that Path becomes a lighted highway of glory and power.

Belief and *praise* and *gratitude,* released in LOVE, bring forth that divine Christ Light from within and permit It to become the great living reality of existence. *Belief* and *praise* and *gratitude,* rayed out on the wings of LOVE, are the three Christ rays that nothing in existence can deter or conquer. No darkness can retard or dim them, no evil overcome them. These three Christ rays, when released, have the power to go instantly and unerringly to the very heart of God. They are the most powerful rays in existence. Within their embrace is contained all the virtues and unutterable, dynamic power of the Kingdom of God.

Belief and *praise* and *gratitude,* when released through LOVE and inner devotion, are the reality of the three divine Christ rays of blue, gold and ruby-red, which contain all the other related colors of the entire spectrum and every divine and holy attribute and trait in living perfection. Therefore, as the divine WHITE Light of Christ is contacted and released, it is transformed from Its original brilliance into the three colorful Christ rays. As they are comprehended and sent out by the individual, they in turn embrace all the other rays and virtues. As they are directed out in flowing currents of vibrant glory direct to the throne of God, they return laden with His power and His fulfillment.

Even as the rainbow in the sky is a token of God's covenant with man in the days of Noah, so is the radiance of the living colors of the spectrum a symbol of God's everlasting covenant to every individual who comes into the world.

When any individual accepts and brings forth that divine White Light of Christ, it is rayed out from him in its developing, variegated colors of vibrational virtues. Thus man fulfills his part of the covenant with God to be noble, obedient and holy, even a divine son. God in turn is *bound* and must fulfill His part of the covenant by bestowing the completed manifestation and power of every holy promise ever made to man by God since time began. The law is irrevocable. This law is the everlasting covenant of God to man. It is "NEW" because it becomes a *new* and breathtaking, glorious, divine experience to every individual who fulfills it. Thus it is known as "The New and Everlasting Covenant".

As man sends out those pure Christ rays, God returns His blessings along them to find their complete fulfillment in the life of him who sent them forth. So it is that the rainbow hues of man's virtues are sent forth on the Light of Christ as It is rayed out in Its varied spectrum from the very heart of man. Thus Christ's holy Light contains the complete power of perfection, redemption and glory as God's personal covenant becomes an established, exalting fulfillment within each man.

When the three Christ rays, blue, gold and ruby-red, are established through *belief, praise* and *gratitude* sent out on the wings of LOVE from the human heart, there is no power in existence which can thwart one's progress and the ultimate fulfilling of all things, for within those three rays are the relative vibrations of every divine virtue.

Along that divine blue Christ ray, as it is sent forth to the very throne of God, to which it travels unerringly, is returned the fulfilling and completion of everything the individual *believes* possible. It is according to the intensity of the blue Christ ray, as it is released from man's own open heart, that God fulfills, or "does His works".

It is now time to reveal fully the divine law by which God's holy Will is fulfilled and all things accomplished.

In using this great and holy law of God one must step beyond the little personal, mortal desires of the outer "self". The little personal desires are only transitory, temporary, physical yearnings fluttering in the bosom of man. These are usually harmful desires and bring only heartaches and unhappiness. They are passing and deceptive and are often only selfish desires. These little mortal cravings of the flesh are either physical, lustful wants, or the desire for worldly wealth or personal power, or the yearnings to be exalted above one's fellowmen. Such desires of the little personal "self" are outgrown and left behind as one fulfills the first and greatest commandment of love toward

God in all its outflowing strength, sent forth from his individual heart, soul and mind.

As one learns to "Be Still" he enters into the holy of holies in the very center of his own soul, where the Light of Christ is concentrated. As he learns to contact that Light by daily effort and practice, he will become purified and cleansed from all sin. This is one of the divine functions of Christ's redeeming Light.

Then as one learns to *abide* in that Light by turning to It constantly, It will be brought forth in Its fullness to fill his entire being. Thus It *abides* in him. "Abide in me and I will abide in you."

It is when one has thus learned to abide in the Christ Light that he becomes filled with Light and begins to comprehend all things. One of the first things revealed and made apparent by the divine Christ Light is the deepest, most intense longing in the individual's own soul. This longing is a holy desire and was implanted in man's center and enfolded in that Christ Light by God Himself at the very beginning of time. It has been lying in embryo, dormant in that living center of man's being, like the germ within the egg. This inner, holy desire, buried and forgotten, is the individual's own personal destiny. That unfulfilled, exalting, divine and eternal pattern of individual accomplishment is the destiny awaiting each man. This exalting, higher destiny is far beyond any personal ambition. This destiny is divine.

It is as one learns to enter that inner stillness within the depths of his own soul, the exalting Christ Light, that he becomes acquainted with God's holy plan awaiting his fulfillment. It is then he has the faith to look clearly and with comprehending vision and realizes that that inner

radiant, exalting destiny has been a crying, yearning, longing part of his own soul from the beginning of time. That
individual destiny and calling is usually far beyond anything one has ever contemplated or dreamed of. At first
it may seem unbelievable and almost overwhelming. The
personal calling may be so dynamically tremendous, so
breathtakingly glorious it may seem impossible to grasp its
full magnitude as one first focuses his attention upon it.

It may be that your own particular calling was never before implanted in the soul of any man. It may be as distinct
and as separate and individual as was the destiny of
Columbus. Nevertheless that destiny was implanted there
by God Himself and it is His Will that it be fulfilled.
Every great, intense *desire of the soul* was implanted there
by God. This must begin to be comprehended as one learns
to discern between the little mortal desires and the destiny
contained within the soul.

It must also be understood here that because there is a
great and holy destiny awaiting each and every man does
not mean that it will be fulfilled. Each man was fore-
ordained to fulfill a certain great and beautiful work, but
he was not predestined to fullfill it. Along with each and
every calling is the gift of free-agency. Man must desire
to fulfill the Will of God and begin to co-operate in doing
his part of the assignment.

As one advances spiritually to the point where he beholds or comprehends his individual destiny, he must develop fully his power to *believe.* He must *believe* in that
inner revelation, that secret vision, that holy destiny crying
within his own soul. He must understand those deep inner
desires which God established within him before the world
was.

As one holds to that divine, inner vision, no matter how seemingly impossible it may appear and *believes* in it, "doubting nothing", it must be fulfilled for it becomes possible through man's *belief*.

As one develops to the point where he *believes* he has the power to send out that blue Christ ray in extending, increasing magnitude. When that ray is united with praise and gratitude, the gold and ruby-red rays, as they are released in LOVE, the three Christ rays unite and reach instantly to the very throne of God. These three rays contain within their vibratory essence the unspeakable Name of Jesus Christ, the great Name of All-power. This Name of infinite glory is Unspeakable simply because it cannot be spoken. It is a vibration! It is the essence and the reality of God's divine power! It is glory unutterable!

Within the blue Christ ray of *belief* the soul's sincere desire is held revealed and open, completely exposed to the divine, fulfilling powers of God. And along that blue ray, as it is beamed out, the inflowing rays of God's Almighty accomplishment is completed as His Will is fulfilled in bringing forth that inner destiny into its outside fulfillment. It is in this way that God's will is done on earth even as it is in heaven. His Will was established in the great hidden destiny enfolded within each man's soul. His Will is fulfilled when man opens his soul to comprehend and through *belief* co-operates in fulfilling his own glorified perfection.

The blue ray is the opened channel of *belief* through which God's holy powers of completion flow back, enfolding the individual destiny and establishing it in glory and honor forever.

This is the law on which faith works. This is how faith

becomes knowing and knowing becomes power! This is the
Way in which His divine, holy Will is fulfilled and the
Way in which the individual glorifies his own destiny. It is
most definitely true that "According to your *belief* be it
unto you"!

Doubting is of the darkness and is the most destructive
weapon of the devil. As long as doubting is permitted to
rule God's works cannot possibly be done, nor His promises
fulfilled. Doubting destroys all things, annihilates all good
and makes all things impossible.

As the Light of Christ is contacted and developed that
divine blue ray is released and sent directly to the glorified
throne of God to make its claim upon Him. And He is
bound and must obey its call, for it was God Himself who
established the covenant. As that divine Christ ray is intensified it carries man's desire to the very heart of God
and it is through this infinite power that one's righteous
desires, his holy ambitions and divine hopes are fulfilled
as the power of God goes into action to complete the request, which He Himself established.

The law, or command to "Ask" also has its part in this
great, breathtaking accomplishment. As one *asks* his own
holy calling becomes clarified to him and is therefore more
rapidly fulfilled. This is the law upon which faith works.
And this law is every man's to use, henceforth and forever.

Again, it must be understood that in using this higher
law it must not be used upon unworthy personal, mediocre,
little, selfish requests. In doing so one is asking amiss and
can be injured by the fulfilling of his own human lusts and
wants.

This divine law of fulfillment is irrevocable when used
to accomplish the Will of God, which is the fulfilling of

each individual's own personal glory and perfection. This is the law of God's eternal covenant with man. It contains the fulfilling of His covenant, both by man and by God. It cannot err. This is the path of glory and of perfection.

To reveal more completely the magnificent glory of God's infinite Good it will be necessary to go one step farther.

That individual pattern, or ordained destiny, locked within that divine Light of Christ is the WORD of God. It is His holy WORD implanted as a promise within each soul. When the quickening, renewing, redeeming Light of Christ is contacted that WORD is given the power of life and will reveal itself as it becomes apparent to the inner consciousness of the individual. When that inner WORD of God is brought forth to its divine fulfillment It is made flesh and the flesh is exalted to the status of the Spirit. This is the law of translation. God's Will is then brought forth onto the physical plane, even as it is established in heaven, the Kingdom within.

That individual pattern or WORD, the holy plan of God for the individual, was sealed or established within the very center of that Christ Light by the Holy Spirit of Promise. This Holy Spirit of Promise is the covenant God made with man before his life on earth ever began.

When the Christ Light is contacted and released through love and becomes established in holiness as one develops the power to *believe* and sends that *belief* forth on the divine Christ ray of blue, that inner promise must be fulfilled.

This inner calling, or WORD of Promise, is the Voice of Christ calling to be heard. When one begins to hear that Voice, or inner WORD, which God spoke into his soul in the beginning, he will open that door to the great Christ Light within. Then it is that the full glory of Christ's

Light will be brought forth and will be sent out in its
glorified spectrum of perfected virtues and attributes to the
very throne of God. Then it is that all things become possible—and all things will be fulfilled in that individual.

Man automatically becomes humble before such powers
and such grandeur. He becomes so humble the little mortal
"self" is lost and dissolved in the great vibrations of praise
and gratitude released in LOVE as he learns to relinquish
his own little personal will to the divine Will of God. It is
in the Will of God that all perfection is held. As the three
divine Christ rays, which contain all the other hues and
vibrational colors, are released the Will of God, which is
enfolded in that inner WORD, begins to be fulfilled as It
is quickened into life and growth—and fulfillment.

This holy WORD, or inner promise, locked in each man's
soul, this inner pattern or divine calling, is the "New and
Everlasting Covenant". This covenant is completely established and must be fulfilled when one no longer rejects
that Light of Christ that has been given to abide in him,
and *believes* in It. As It is accepted in loving praise and
gratitude It is released to begin Its process of fulfilling
glory. When that Light is accepted the three Christ rays
are released, and as they are strengthened and beamed out
in power, the virtues of all the living rays of the rainbow
reach the throne of God. The sending out of these rays is
man's part of the New and Everlasting Covenant.

When those rays reach the throne of God, He must of
necessity fulfill His part of that Covenant. He must bring
forth that inner WORD by the very glory of His power.
God is actually bound by that covenant and when man
fulfills his part of it and overcomes his evils by accepting
the holy Christ Light as he rays It back to God in Its spec-

trumed vibrations of increasing virtues, God must fulfill His part of that covenant. God must accept those rays and return the power of His approbation to complete the fulfilling and perfection of that individual's destiny. This is the law and it is irrevocable. It cannot err, nor can it fail.

When any individual's destiny is accomplished and fulfilled it will be for the eternal glory of God and will also be for the benefit of all concerned.

No man who fulfills this holy law by first accepting that divine Christ Light, given to abide within him, then raying it out, can possibly remain under condemnation. He is not only redeemed, but is exalted and glorified.

The rainbow has always held the symbol of this eternal, everlasting covenant. The rainbow in the sky is just a reminder of that eternal symbol and inner covenant. It is only the dim reproduction, or semblance of that which man must establish through his own glorified vibrations of increasing virtues as the Light of Christ is accepted. The first of the Christ rays is *belief*. Only through the power to *believe* can the other rays be established. Without *belief* nothing can be accomplished.

It can be stated here that the saying, "At the foot of the rainbow is the pot of gold" is definitely true. At the foot of those rays as they are released within man is the great Christ Light, the realm of Spirit, the purified gold which has been tried in the fire.

Those who *believe* in and accept that divine "Light of Christ, which has been given to abide in every man who cometh into the world," will be led to fulfill their part of that holy Covenant and cannot possibly remain under condemnation, or in darkness. Their mediocrity drops away as they become filled with Light and are made glorious.

Because this Way has been an inner Way the churches and groups of the past have not traveled it. They have traveled instead the outside road of orthodox conformity and of set rituals as "They have honored God with their lips, while their hearts have been far from Him".

The Light of Christ must be comprehended and brought forth from within man in order to prepare for the glorious, triumphant coming of the Lord of Lords and King of Kings, even Jesus Christ Himself, to rule and reign in glory and honor upon this earth. But before this greatest of all events can happen there must be those who are prepared to receive Him, those who have brought forth His Light within themselves. These are the ones who "Will be like Him when He appears, for they will be purified, even as He is pure!" Within them will the WORD of God have been made flesh as they stand forth redeemed and sanctified.

"These will be filled with His holy Light and will comprehend all things."

This inner Way is the Way of the Christ Light that Jesus traveled. It is a straight and narrow Way in that it does not lead out into many diversified courses of mortal inclinations. It is the Way of unspeakable power, glory and infinite, individual achievement. It is the Way of boundless joy and of overcoming. It is the Way of purification, of redemption and of exalting glory. It is the Way that perfects all things and fulfills all things as it leads one to the Father—even to His Fullness.

The Christ Way is the road of exaltation. In this Path one is not even burdened or concerned by the ugly, defiled traits and desires for they are automatically overcome as one learns to hold himself within Christ's redeeming Light. In this Way, which is His, can one be purified, cleansed, redeemed and completely glorified.

The Christ Way is the Path of honor and praise and unutterable beauty. It is the Way of power and loving redemption, though so few have ever found it. It is the way that leads to the great Christ Door of Eternal Life, where death and its accompanying sorrows, suffering, woes and ugliness is unknown. It is the road of triumphant overcoming. And there is no individual upon this earth who cannot travel it, if he so desires. "The Light of Christ is given to abide in every man who cometh into the world." And this Christ Light IS the Way.

The Christ Light is also the great corner stone of His power. It is the stone on which man, who is the temple of God, was established. It is also the stone that was rejected by the builders as man built his physical body. Nevertheless It is the corner stone of divine power and eternal, Celestial, magnificent grandeur and power. And he who builds upon this rock, of His Light, cannot fail—or fall. The Light of Christ is the white stone, which is established in power by him who accepts It, leaving his mortal inclinations behind which yearn for the broad, open way of the multitudes—the road that leads to destruction. And in that stone, or Light, a new Name is written and none can know that Name saving he who is worthy to receive It for It can be given to none except those who travel His holy Way of Light as they are directed by His leading.

This holy, Christ Way is a Way of such unutterable glory, such divine, infinite joy, such unspeakable power there are no words in any language to express it. "It is the Way Christ marked—the Way He traveled." It is the Way that releases the power of God so that I can *do the works,* and fulfill Its holy promises to all those who *believe.*

You hesitate and say that Christ's path led to the crucifixion?

Yes. That is true. But the crucifixion became a privileged experience of triumph and eternal blessing, not only to Christ, but to the whole world and to every individual upon it. The Way of Christ holds the power to turn every adversity into glory, every defeat into victory, every misfortune into power. It is the road of love, so perfect that only the Will of the Father is brought forth in Its triumphant glory as the little individual, mortal "self" is crucified and the great inner soul of man is released from its tomb, to rule and reign in glory forever.

This divine Way of Christ is the Way that fulfills all things, glorifies and exalts all things. "Behold, I stand at the door and knock. If any man hear my voice and open that door, I will come in and feast with him, and he with me." And that individual will never hunger or thirst again. He will have eternal access to the hidden manna, the divine, spiritual "Bread of Life". And Christ's Light that is given to abide right within man IS that bread.

"To my beloved ones, the Spirit and the bride say, Come. And let him that heareth say, Come. And let him that is athirst come. And whosoever will, let him take of the waters of life freely," without price and without charge.

THE GREAT ETERNAL NOW—
THE POINT OF POWER

Chapter XVIII

Negative conditions are the raw materials out of which the enlightened man builds. If one is thankful in all things he recognizes no negation. He knows that all things or conditions are but blessings in reverse. He knows also that with the proper understanding and the right attitude they can be immediately transformed into their true, beneficial purposes. Every little nerve-wracking irritation, every resentful thought, every discordant vibration can be instantly converted and transformed into released power through the stilled reflection of a calm and love-filled mind.

To the enlightened one, even the loss of all his wealth and possessions holds no bleak dismay. He comprehends that seeming misfortunes and reverses are blessings in disguise, if he accepts them as such. He understands fully that the removal of his physical, worldly holdings is but the discarding of his worn-out apparel. As his outer trappings are removed he is prepared to be clothed in holy raiment and arrayed in Light.

So it is that the enlightened one can rejoice in what may completely destroy another. This is because the enlightened one uses every incident, every condition, every setback by transforming the negative powers contained within them into good and into blessings. If the enlightened one is stripped

243

of every tangible thing he possesses he knows that the power contained in such reverses can be immediately used for the sanctification of his soul as he uses them to release the infinite powers contained within. Every loss that is met by an individual in this attitude contains illimitable power.

It is impossible to comprehend this indescribable power unless one is willing to let go of every possession and every tie and hold of mortality and live by the knowledge of the inward working of the higher law. "Live it and you will know of its truth"—and of its power.

There is no evil condition to the awakened one for he knows the law and uses it aright. No resentment or negation can touch him, no calamity disturbs him. Thus he converts the energies contained within the adverse conditions into the powers of fulfilling glory. These energies could be likened to entities. They are forces of power and are subject to command. They are the "Legions" which go instantly to work for the man who has purified himself by bringing forth that Divine Christ Light from within.

There are many types of losses. All may become blessings if they have not been brought on by deliberate wickedness, stupidity or callous rebelliousness. And even then these negative forces can be converted and transformed when one is ready to open his mind to comprehend.

One of the most difficult losses to sustain is the loss of one's own deeply embedded ideas or accepted beliefs. Those who are big enough to face the loss of their own set opinions when proved erroneous are prepared for speedy advancement. Usually the loss of one's faith in some embedded idea is quite shattering at first. It is the man who has the ability and versatility to gather up his forces and rebuild upon new truth who is prepared to walk in Light.

The individual who is true enough and advanced enough to be willing to give up some personal, petty want or selfish desire and turn it over to the mind and will of God places himself upon a higher level. This is the level in which the fulfilling powers of God can become operative in his life.

As one advances into this state of loving acceptance, or becomes willing to accept adversities and meet vicissitudes and negative issues with gratitude and love, such conditions will be transmuted into power and blessings almost instantly. This one has "learned obedience by the things he has suffered" and for him all suffering ends.

All negative conditions and even the most undesirable things imaginable are the materials of unutterable glory to the individual who recognizes them for what they are, the raw materials of life which are placed in his hands. These are the materials the wise man converts and uses as he builds the visions his soul aspires to. These seemingly harsh, raw, unwieldly materials are the materials of unspeakable power and ineffable blessings when they are transmuted by the glory of His Light, which is always expressed in superior understanding. Ignorance is darkness. Understanding and knowledge are Light.

Any individual who uses his negative circumstances and reverse conditions with this knowledge will become glorious. His very ability to accept and give thanks and praise and honor and glory to God for these conditions will release the glorifying, fulfilling powers of God and set those powers into immediate action. And that individual who uses his troubles in this manner is making the "right-use" of the laws of God's Kingdom and will himself become glorious. The "right-use" of these powers is true righteousness!

These higher powers and blessings cannot be used by the

self-righteous, nor can they be used by the weak, resentful individual, or the one who dully accepts his burdens as the will of God. Sorrow, failure, misery, distress, darkness and suffering are never the will of God! And only the weak individual is willing to permit such conditions to mar and destroy his life. To the enlightened, understanding one no condition is a burden. It is an opportunity. To the enlightened one no difficulty or adverse condition can possibly become a weight of paralyzing hopelessness. It is those who writhe in helpless self-pity who not only live in the negation of their seeming reverses but who actually open up their arms to such conditions as they gather them in. To such the burdens of dismaying evils are accepted and falsely acclaimed to be the will of God. Such acclamations are blasphemy. The will of God holds naught but beauty, loveliness, power and glory. And he whose life contains none of these things is out of tune with the divine will of God. His eyes have never been lifted to the heights to behold the glory of God, nor has his vision been adjusted to become "single to that glory"!

All that is required to release these transforming powers of Almighty God into one's life is the willingness to accept the loss of all that one might possess, whether it be just decaying, worldly possessions, corroding negation, destructive hates, dismaying worries, intolerable suffering or annihilating fears. As these powers of negation and darkness are released, or let go of, they can be transmuted, transformed, converted or translated into their rightful use. These powers, when converted and refined, are the divine powers of construction—not destruction.

There are only two requisites necessary in order to be able to use these great powers of transition. The first

requisite is the power to *believe.* The second is the ability
to use, or *LIVE* by the use of the higher law.

"He who is thankful in all things shall be made glorious;
and the things of this earth shall be added unto him a
hundredfold; yea, more!" Whatever one sustains in his
losses, as he takes hold of the higher laws, will be returned
to him a hundredfold—and more. The conditions will be
lifted from darkness and negation into glory and light and
power. Man's own singing song of gratitude truly has the
power to make him glorious, if he will only use it in released thanksgiving.

The individual who lives these higher laws and who uses
them correctly is no longer the pawn of destiny or the
creature of circumstances; he is the master of them.

To such, all things and all conditions "Become subject
unto him; both in heaven and on earth; the life and the
light, the Spirit and the power, sent forth by the Will of
the Father, through Jesus Christ, His Son".

Every tiny, irritating condition or personal inefficacy, as
well as every calamity or major tragedy can be thus transformed into inexpressible power and glory as one becomes
transmuted, translated by his own attitudes into a new creature, love-filled and glorious.

"He who is thankful in all things" opens up the fountains
of joy right within his own soul. This is the source of contact with the "Fountain of Living waters".

"The Fountain of Living Water" is the permanent, flowing, joyous ecstasy of the Spirit. It is the released glory contained within the Great Christ Light. As one learns to contact and use this great inner source of singing gratitude and
joyous life all negation and darkness is transformed into
blessings. In this singing gratitude and joy the Christ Light

is contacted and released and one is prepared to receive even "A Fullness of Joy" or a "Fullness of the Father". And this joy becomes a permanent factor as one becomes filled with Light, or knowledge and understanding—hence, power.

All sorrows and negation, all misery and distress, all pain and suffering are but the fruits of the "Tree of Good and Evil", rendering its "good" as "evil" to him who either breaks or ignores the right use of the law, or who remains ignorant of it. Within man is the power to transform the evil into good, transmute the bitter into sweet and exalt the darkness and negation into Light and glory and divine power.

Man is either the master or the slave, according to his attitude, his ignorance or his degree of enlightenment.

Man is the one who decides how he will use the raw materials of life that are placed within his hands. This ancient scripture expresses it beautifully: "I gave men weaknesses that they might become strong." In the weaknesses is contained the energy to become not only strong, but mighty. Within the weaknesses is contained the raw material, the stored energy of illimitable power. He who uses the raw materials of life correctly will soon be given only the pure, refined, glorified materials of God and they will not require man's energies to re-process and refine them. They will be the direct forces of God, "The Light and the Life, the Spirit and powers of creation in their fully glorified state". As man overcomes the darkness, his evils and jealousies and becomes humble, these divine forces do become subject unto him, even as God promised they would be.

The powers of fulfilling are timed by man's ability to turn *belief* into *faith,* which is always power in action. This is accomplished when one is able to transfer his hopes for the future into the reality of the present. This is entirely within the hands of the individual and will come to pass whenever he is ready.

Man contacts the powers of God through the super-conscious mind. Anything that has been placed within the super-conscious mind through habit, belief or fear becomes a reality. Because of this God-given factor within man to choose whether he will use his divine forces for good or evil, the world is in the condition that it has reached today. The super-conscious mind has been fed upon negation and hates and it has returned the darkness thereof into the lives of men. No one has desired this condition. It has been created through ignorance and a rejection of the great Christ Light.

The things one thinks, feels or does release the creative forces of this super-conscious mind and they become realities. Negative thinking and feeling habits bring forth negative conditions into one's life and into the world. Whatever thoughts or emotions one sends into his super-conscious mind become the living factors and the realities of his daily life.

The Light of Christ, as it is developed and brought forth, contains the power to cleanse and purify the super-conscious of its accumulated negative gatherings, its hidden fears, jealousies, resentments and lusts that have been compressed into its recesses from the time the conscious mind became active. Within the Christ Light is the power of regeneration and redemption for man as both the conscious and the super-conscious minds are filled with Christ's purifying, redeeming, glorifying Light.

It is the right and the purpose of the conscious mind to

direct and use the unspeakable powers of that divine super-conscious mind at all times. When the conscious mind knowingly and with awakened understanding directs the super-conscious mind, all the great, indescribable promises of the Almighty must be fulfilled in all their perfection. This is the method that brings all things and conditions as well as all powers into subjection. And "All things will be subject unto him, both in heaven and on earth; the Life and the Light, the Spirit and the power", etc. But it must be understood that the powers contained within the great super-conscious mind "doeth the works", or contact the direct powers of God to accomplish all things. This divine mind, when purified, is always in direct contact with God at all times—and with His powers. So it is that "all that the Father has is yours"!

Within this great super-conscious mind is contained the keys of this glorious passage of ancient scripture: "It is given to abide in you, the record of heaven; the Comforter; the peaceable things of immortal glory; the truth of all things; that which quickeneth all things, and maketh alive all things; that which knoweth all things, and hath all power."

"The Light of Christ has also been given to abide in every man who cometh into the world". . . . . "Yea, all that the Father has is yours!"

When the Light of Christ is no longer a rejected factor the hardness of the heart will be completely melted and love and tenderness, goodness and mercy will fill one's being. With that redeeming Light active the blindness of the mind will be removed.

These higher promises and laws are completed and fulfilled in that first and greatest of all commandments.

To love God with all one's heart opens up that divine heart-center to love and to the great Christ-Light, which IS the Fountain of Life.

To love God with all one's soul is the process by which the physical body is quickened and renewed. The cells are regenerated and spiritualized and the whole being is quickened and redeemed and glorified.

To love God with all one's mind is the power which unites the conscious mind and the super-conscious mind and they begin to function as ONE. As they are thus united by love there is nothing either in heaven or on earth that is impossible for love is established and its pure perfection resuscitates and makes alive all things.

In this released, perfected, divine love man himself is the benefactor. It is in this great love that the "Atonement" for which Christ gave His life is completed. This is the great "At-one-ment" when the Light of Christ, the conscious and super-conscious minds of man blend and become ONE in a new and divine power of functioning.

When man comprehends the illimitable powers contained right within himself, when the conscious mind knowingly and with its Christ enlightened understanding opened, works with the great inner, spiritual mind of infinite power, nothing is impossible.

One's progress always commences with his ability to believe. Doubts are the released powers of determent, negation and destruction as they hold back and retard the forces of Light. Ignorance is the imbecilic child of doubting. It is a creature of darkness and is often completely blind. It is usually bigoted and often cruel. *Belief,* on the other hand is the child of divine power and will grow into *faith* when it is nurtured and fed. *Belief* must be cared for in order for it to grow and mature.

When *belief* is established, *doubt* is banished and its evil, malformed, degenerate spawn, Ignorance.

Belief, however, is still an imperfect factor. It is but a child. Its one purpose and function is to counteract and overcome *doubt.* In this capacity it is perfect and beautiful. After *belief* has fulfilled the purpose of its childhood it matures into *faith. Belief* grows into *faith. Faith* matures into *knowledge*—and *knowledge is power.*

Faith contains the power to develop into *know.* It is in *faith* that the active forces of fulfillment are established. *Belief* is an immature child, though very desirable and very beautiful and very necessary. *Belief* is not too powerful. It is almost inactive, except for its ability to keep *doubt* from becoming established in its place. However when *belief* matures into *Faith* it develops the power of action. *Belief* is the small child learning to walk. *Faith* is the child matured into youth as it enters eagerly into active service to release dynamic powers.

In *faith* is the power of fulfilling brought forth. This is the nature and manner of *faith.*

Paul understood the truth behind the powers of God when he stated simply and humbly, "We believe all things!" There are very few who have even that infant power to *believe.* These are the ones who question and rend all truth and who have no power within them except to doubt.

Belief, the child, places all fulfillment and hope out into the future. *Faith* establishes it in the NOW. *Belief* extends the prayer or the hope into the realm of "becoming". *Faith* establishes it in the present. The *become* is transformed

into the HERE and NOW. With the power of this trans-
formation *faith* becomes *knowing* and *knowledge is power*—
the power of all fulfillment.

The super-conscious mind always works in the NOW.
When the "at-one-ment" is established between the conscious and the great super-conscious minds one steps into
the NOW—the eternal PRESENT. The fulfilling power is
always in the NOW. The vague, distant vision of *belief* or
hope for the future becomes completed in the great, living,
dynamic, all-powerful NOW!

The great, ever-present NOW is the eternal. It is the
point of power. He who continues to hold his hopes out
into the future for fulfillment is still using but the infant
child, *belief* instead of its matured, powerful expression,
faith.

Nevertheless the one who holds steadfastly to his power
to *believe,* who refuses doubt admittance, will himself grow
into the power of *faith.* He who holds to *belief* with determined tenacity will soon cease to abide in the lesser
phase of power but will advance automatically into the
dynamic, fulfilling glory of *faith.* In this growth and transition one's vision is drawn in from the distant view and is
focused upon the powerful, ever-present NOW.

This great, living power of the NOW is what Christ was
seeking to reveal when He said, "Take no thought for
tomorrow."

NOW is as much a part of eternity as all the yesteryears
of the past and the great tomorrows of the future. But it
is only in the NOW that the powers of eternity are active
and of benefit. And it is only in the NOW that one can
ever have contact with the great Light of Christ and the
Almighty power of God.

The fulfilling power of every hope and every worthy desire is waiting in the NOW. As one re-focuses his vision for the future upon the glory of the present, *belief* is transformed into *faith*. *Faith* is always an active power and establishes the fulfilling ingredient that completes and brings forth. *Faith* always grows into *knowledge*. And *knowledge is power.* When one *knows,* he has the ability and the understanding to *do!* The power to *do* is always contained in the NOW!

Whatever can be, already has the power to be. All perfection, all glory and goodness and beauty and abundance is in the divine NOW.

When one can lift his vision and his prayers from the plea, "Let me *become* love" or "Let me *become* this" or "that" or "the other" into the NOW, he can say "I *am* love! I *am* filled with Light! I *am* endowed with the powers of Almighty God, my Father, as God performs His works through me!" . . . . . 'And it is so! Even as he saith!" . . . . . "Yea, all that the Father has *IS* yours!"

This truth has always been so. Because man could not lift his "eyes" or vision to the glory of God he could not behold it except "through a glass darkly" or dimly, or off in the future. By *faith* that veil is removed and the dim vision that was extended out into the future becomes the reality of the NOW!

NOW is your appointed time to take hold of these blessings and to become powerful!

Think it NOW! Live it NOW! Know that it is NOW and the great veils of darkness shall be dissolved before your eyes.

It may take a little time for one to re-focus his eyes to

this great, perfect reality. But he who can learn to adjust his eyes and thoughts to abide in the Eternal NOW of fulfilling power will no longer be subjected to either time or space. In these three steps, from *belief* to *faith* to *knowing,* learn to place your petitions, not in the future for fulfillment, but in the NOW. Your hopes and requests and noble desires must always be held in the NOW! And you must live as though they were already fulfilled. The NOW is the point of contact! The NOW is the place of power! The NOW holds the keys of all fulfillment and of glorious completion! The NOW is the point where the hope of the future becomes the established fulfillment of the present.

Live NOW as though you already had the complete fulfillment of your worthy desires. Live NOW as though you were this love! Live NOW as though you were arrayed in Light and verily it shall be according as you yourself designate. You are the one who sets the time. It is established according to your *belief* in the future, or your active *Faith* and its powers contained always in the present—the eternal NOW!

ASK, then immediately give thanks that your request has been heard! Then leave it to God to work out. This principle is best portrayed when Christ raised Lazarus from the dead. "And Jesus lifted up his eyes, and said, Father, I thank thee that thou hast heard me. And I knew that thou hearest me always: but because of the people which stand by I said it, that they may believe that thou hast sent me. And when he thus had spoken, he cried with a loud voice, Lazarus, come forth. And he that was dead came forth!" Note that Christ gave thanks to God for having heard His prayer before it was fulfilled. Giving thanks and praise establishes it in the NOW!

Just know always that your prayer is heard. Hold yourself open and in ready preparation to receive the answer. And It will come. Give thanks always for the answer to your prayers, the fulfilling of your holy desires, the nearness of God and for His power being released into your life. As your requests are established in love the great fulfilling laws of God are put into operation. These holy, divine laws of God are irrevocable and cannot err or fail. Release all you have hoped for into the great ever-present NOW and give thanks and it will return to you fulfilled in a more beautiful way than your greatest hope ever envisioned, your highest dream ever imagined or your most intense yearning ever conceived.

In using this power remember to walk humbly, for these powers are the powers of God as He begins to do His works, through you. And God will not be mocked. Worship and adore and give thanks and as you send out love humility will be exalted. Humility, purified and contrite is the power of reception. Humility is a vital force. It is the irresistible point of contact when one learns to let go and let God take over. The little strident, pride-filled mortal self, that has caused so much suffering learns the perfect obedience through the superb gift of divine humility. It is when pride steps aside that God is permitted to step forth with His healing powers of perfection and infinite joy and exalting glory.

Let love become the pulsebeat of your existence. Let singing gratitude and praise and adoration vibrate out from your soul continually and you will never become blinded by the brilliance of His Light, nor be singed by the Cosmic

Rays of His fulfilling powers as they become visible to your eyes.

Through the singing song of love in your soul, through gratitude and adoring contrition of heart the keys of all power will become operative in your life. And you will be glorious!

THE LIGHT OF NOONDAY

Chapter XIX

The books I have written have been written because this was my destiny and because God commanded it. These books have been sent forth without price or royalties, on my part, that all could receive them at the lowest possible cost. They were not written to obtain money or fame or credit or reward. They were written wholly for the glory of God and for the benefit and enlightenment of man. I have written with a pen dipped in heaven and the writings are engraved with the flame of eternal truth. This flame of Truth, or Light of Christ, will consume the veils of darkness for those who desire to overcome the blindness and receive sight and vision. And the way will be opened for those who desire to be quickened and made alive—if they will only *believe*—, or who will humbly ask God to help their *unbelief*.

By these records, by our lives and yours, you noble and awakened ones, shall the sins of many generations be overcome and the darkness of the ages be dispelled.

It is noonday and there are many who are still walking in darkness because of the great blindness of mind which has been caused because of *unbelief* or is the direct result of men trusting in the "arm of flesh" as "the blind", or those without vision or spiritual contact "are leading the blind".

The blind are those who have never comprehended "The divine Light of Christ that has been given to abide in every man who cometh into the world".

The Light of God is being released in increasing brilliance upon the earth. It is blinding to those who have conformed their lives to the darkness as they have ignorantly rejected that Christ Light and so have remained under condemnation. Often the great blindness has been caused by a refusal to open the eyes to look. "There are none so blind as those who will not see."

"The blind leaders of the blind" are fighting against God and realize it not. Their zeal may be as great as was the zeal of Saul of Tarsus and as harmful and injurious.

The Light of Christ is the light of noonday and is becoming daily more apparent as those with vision, those who are not blind, are bringing It forth. This very Light of Christ has the power to dispel the darkness of the ages. This Light is becoming so powerful that those who are not wilfully blind will begin "to see out of obscurity and out of blindness".

"Those who are walking in the darkness at noonday" because they love the darkness rather than the light, cannot possibly believe or imagine that God is a God of power, or a God of miracles. They love the great mist accumulated by the ages and the darkness that veils all truth in the unholy worship of the past. They believe it is blasphemy to lift one's eyes to behold the glory of God. These "blind leaders of the blind" and their zealous followers would destroy all who dare to believe in the path Christ trod and who follow it. They mentally stone to death those who behold in the promises of the scripture the possibility of God literally fulfilling His promises. They burn at the stake, in effigy at least, those who, in beholding the promises and the glory of God, believe that man was meant to be perfect, even as God is perfect! They shout in protest and gnash their teeth against the idea of this scripture meaning what it says: "Let the same mind be in you which was in Christ Jesus; who being in the form of God thought it not robbery to be equal with God." And in the blindness of their zeal they defile the exalted throne of God to disprove Christ's teachings which proclaim "that *all* who believe in Him would have the power to do the works which He did—even greater works"!

These pathetic, misdirected, blind ones may have their physical minds filled with earthly wisdom and scholarly, mortal knowledge and such learning may only have increased their blindness. The blindness of mind caused by the great wickedness of *unbelief,* is the blindness that cannot behold the things of the Spirit but only the tangible, gross, physical things of the flesh—the things of which their five weak little mortal senses bear witness. These blind ones believe they are sanctified because they have conformed their lives to a few narrow, orthodox principles, not realizing that rigid *conformity* to blind, powerless rituals brings only *deformity* of soul as it intensifies one's blindness.

It is the blind who cleanse with meticulous, fanatical care the outside of the cup, but who remain filthy and unclean within. No one can possibly commence to cleanse the inside of the cup, which is himself, without beginning to comprehend the Light of Christ entombed in his own inner being. And as that Light is comprehended it must come forth and bring with it the brightness of noonday and its fulfilling and completing powers of enlightening glory.

The blindly zealous profess Christ in their words, but their works and their actions and their lives decry their belief by their lack of power. "The blind leaders of the blind" are often the ones who are most lost in darkness, as they lead their followers into the great ditch. And those who are willing to follow such blind leaders, who have no other power than to preach their great sermons of words, are trusting in the arm of flesh instead of in the power of God and in their own contact with Him and His power, hence they too remain blind. Any man is blind who has not the direct contact with God through that divine Christ Light which has been given to abide in him.

The lost, blind ones accept every law of the flesh willingly and eagerly as they cloak their sins and selfishness, their greeds and lusts, prides, jealousies and fears, their unquenchable cravings for power and pomp and acclaim behind their whitewashed robes. Their sanctimonious lip worship fills the whole earth while "Their hearts are far from Him".

No man can possibly turn his heart to God fully without discovering the great Christ Light. And in that Light is contained all power, all truth, all love and the power to heal the blindness of mind. This Christ Light contains all that is necessary to cleanse and purify and redeem any individual who will only accept It and let It direct his life into peace and power and fulfillment. This Light of Christ IS the great glorious Light of noonday. This Light reveals all that the darkness of midnight obscured and concealed.

There are thousands who are no longer blind! These awakened ones are finding the great inner Light of Christ as they are beginning to tread the path He mapped—the path that leads one into the great noonday Light of all-knowing. These enlightened ones are preparing to usher in the great New Day—the day of His glory and His power as they are purifying themselves to prepare the world for His coming.

It must be fully comprehended here that Christ cannot appear to any individual or group who is unpurified and uncleansed. "When he appears we will be like him!" . . . . . "We will be purified even as He is pure!" That is, if one is to have a part in His glory and abide in His day. Deny this and you deny Him and in so doing will never have the power to be accepted into His Kingdom—which Kingdom is at hand.

These great ones have the ability and the adjusted vision to look directly into that Light and to behold the breathtaking wonder of the glory of God and in that exalted vision "Their eyes become single to that glory". In such exalted vision one comprehends the purpose of his own existence and his relationship to God as he steps forth into the Light to fulfill the promises of Jesus Christ in all their glory and to do the works which He did—even the greater works!

"The eye that must become single to the glory of God" is the eye of one's attention. It is the centering of one's awareness upon the power of God. When one's attention is centered upon God and His glory instead of upon outside things, he will grow into that glory. He becomes filled with love and praise and gratitude and he who is thankful in all things will be made glorious! He will become like that which he gazes upon. No one can possibly have "eyes single to the glory of God" and trust in a vengeful, powerless, mediocre God, nor one that is so far remote and removed from himself it would be impossible to contact Him. When one's eyes become single to the glory of God, God begins to be comprehended in all His dynamic glory of fulfilling power and infinite love. Anyone who thus comprehended God begins to bring forth those divine qualities within himself, for God will unveil His face to such.

The seed of each man's perfection and glory and power is contained within that divine, holy Christ Light. This sacred, unfulfilled seed contained within man is the seed of divinity. It is the seed of God Himself. This holy power of life is dormant and unfulfilled until the individual himself begins to do his own asking, his own seeking and his own searching or begins to desire to know God. As one hungers and thirsts after righteousness, after that sacred, inner food that will feed and develop his soul, he will be brought to that Christ Light and begin to comprehend it. Man himself must begin that great search in order to make his own contact with the Light of Christ, which is indeed the bread of life!

Until man begins to seek to know and comprehend God through that direct, personal search, which is the inward path, instead of through outward forms, he could be compared to a seed that is unquickened and dormant. Man himself can be best compared to the outside shell of a seed, an acorn, a chestnut, or even an egg in which the potential life forces have not been quickened into vitalizing life. Man, with all his outside activity, is but his own impotent factors of existence being expressed while the germ or inner life forces of himself lie lifeless, unawakened and undeveloped and unfulfilled.

When the Light of Christ is contacted that seed is made

alive, or is quickened into life and growth. With that quickening the seed of God begins Its development. The great *immaculate* conception has already taken place. That divine seed of God was implanted within man in the very beginning. This divinely implanted seed of God is the holy, misunderstood, immaculate conception. And each and every soul is a bearer of that potential Sonship, or Christhood. Man is the container of that seed of God. When that "Light of Christ, which is given to abide in every man who cometh into the world" is contacted, through man's love and desiring and hungering and thirsting after righteousness, that life-center of God's own embryoed divinity is quickened into life and growth and he who contains that awakened spark or germ of divinity will be prepared to be born of God.

"But as many as received Him (Christ, or the Christ Light), to them gave he power to become the sons of God, even to them that believe on His Name (or His Light); which were born, not of blood, nor of the will of the flesh, nor of the will of man, but of God." (John 1:13).

"Whosoever is born of God doth not commit sin; for his seed remaineth in him: and he cannot sin, because he is born of God." (I John 3:9).

"Beloved, let us love one another: for love is of God; and everyone that loveth is born of God." (I John 4:7).

"If we receive the witness of men, the witness of God is greater; for this is the witness of God which he hath testified of His Son. He that believeth on the Son of God *hath the witness in himself* (even the Light of Christ): he that believeth not God hath made him a liar; because he believeth not the record God gave of his Son. And this is the record, that God hath given to us eternal Life, and this life is in the Son. He that hath the Son hath life; and he that hath not the Son of God hath not life." (I John 5:9-12). He who does not have this Light of Christ does not have the gift of eternal life and is subject unto death.

"I am the true vine, and my Father is the husbandman. Every branch in me that beareth not fruit he taketh away: and every branch that beareth fruit, he purgeth it, that it may bring forth more fruit . . . . . Abide in me, and I in you. As the branch cannot bear fruit of itself, except it abide in the vine; no more can ye, except ye abide in me. I am the vine, ye are the branches: He that abideth in me, and I in him, the same bringeth forth much fruit: for without me ye can do nothing. If a man abide not in me, he is cast forth as a branch, and is withered; and men gather them, and cast them into the fire, and they are burned. If ye abide in me, and my words abide in you, ye shall ask what ye will; and it shall be done unto you." (John 15:1-7).

The only possible way Christ could be the vine is through that Christ Light contained within man. This vine furnishes the supply of spiritual food necessary for growth and development and production. Know this, the branches are as necessary to the vine as the vine is to the branches. They must work together as ONE.

"At that day ye shall *know* that I Am in my Father, and ye in me, and I in you!" (John 14:20). At that day, when man contacts that Christ Light within himself and brings it forth, he will *know* the truth and the power of the foregoing scripture. He will realize that without that contact with Christ's holy Light he is as impotent and lifeless as a dead and worthless branch, as unfulfilled as a seed that has not been quickened into life, as dormant as the egg in which the embryoed germ has not been awakened to partake of its supply of food that it might fulfill its individual destiny.

Physical, mortal man is as unregenerate, ineffective, unstimulated, inexpedient, unredeemed and unquickened and powerless as any seed that remains dormant and unfulfilled. Physical man is but the outside container of that divine seed of God as it awaits the quickening warmth of love in Christ's awakening Light. As that Light of Christ is contacted the divine seed of God is quickened and held out, exposed to the great fulfilling rays of God's Almighty, completing powers and it must come forth in all its glorified perfection. This completion is man himself, redeemed, perfected, glorified and powerful—a Son of God.

Without the contact with that divine Christ Light man is an impotent creature, abiding in darkness. He is powerless though he creates machinery that can destroy the world, memorizes all collected, worldly knowledges (which is but foolishness to the Lord) or travels to the moon. Yet man himself becomes daily more the creature of circumstances, the slave of earth's environment, the puny man of flesh engulfed in his mean little personal weaknesses and problems as he is tossed by every vicissitude.

When, through the Light of Christ, man evolves into the heretofore embryoed powers implanted within his being he is no longer a slave, but a master. Such divine ones cannot be storm-tossed or mediocre, nor are they impotent and powerless. They are majestic sons of God, crowned with divinity.

And the time is NOW!

As one lives the higher Christ laws they become his to use in all their released power and glory.

It is noonday and the Light of Christ is being comprehended, being released through the hearts and souls of men as His promises and powers are becoming manifest in the lives of those who follow His path. All who deny His words and His powers are actually denying Him though they realize it not.

This is the day when all men will be left without excuse. The day and time of excuses has been left behind in the darkness. In the great Light there is no need or possibility for excuses, for that which is Perfect is come.

The path Christ trod is so plainly marked a fool need not err therein. All that is necessary is that one *believe* in the things He taught—*believe* in the promises He gave and *live* the laws He revealed.

It is not a difficult road. It is most simple and easy. All righteousness and all powers, every law is contained and fulfilled in the living of the two great commandments.

Permit me again to point out the glory and the power and the wonder of these laws of His great revealing Light.

As one loves God with all his heart the hard seal which has closed up that great heart-center is broken. When that hard seal is broken the heart is left open and melted. As this condition of the broken or unsealed, melted heart is achieved the Christ Light is revealed and begins to be made manifest.

It must also be remembered that the broken, or opened heart is the only acceptable sacrifice. It is the only offering man can possibly render that is worthy of the Lord. It was appointed unto man as the offering supreme in the days of Christ, our Lord. No other offering is acceptable. Only this melted, open, tender, contrite heart is worthy of the divine gift of Christ's released, holy Light. This offering or sacrifice of the heart humbles and dissolves all pride, arrogance, hardness and self-will. This is the only gift worthy of acceptance at the throne of God.

One's life, wealth, energies, time or talents, as they are offered in pride and bigotry, have only power to render some outside, mediocre service. By the great inner offering of a broken heart, which can only be achieved through loving God with *all* one's heart, the supreme, acceptable sacrifice is rendered. Then only is it possible for the Light of Christ to direct one's services that they be neither wasted nor in vain. Only this broken, or open heart, as it releases the great Christ Light from within, has power and is worthy and acceptable as It fulfills the holy law God requires to glorify one's life.

As the great broken or open heart-center of man's own being is opened through love, the entombed Christ Light is released. This "Christ Light has been given to abide in every man who cometh into the world". And within that Christ Light is contained the embryoed seed of God waiting to be brought forth in its perfection to make man himself divine. This Christ Light, when released, is the great revealing Light of noonday and one becomes filled with that Light and comprehends all things and receives all power. Within this divine Christ Light is the power of Life Eternal, for only in this Light and by It can one comprehend and know God. Within this divine Light are the powers of forgiveness and redemption and the powers of complete purification as one's sins and weaknesses, errors and mistakes are cleansed and purified by Its released, ineffable, redemptive powers.

Those who are blind because of the great wickedness of *unbelief*, will deny this Light of Christ, or falsely claim they possess it when they do not. Many believe they have a special monolopy upon Christ's Light even while they are rejecting it more violently than any others. This is the cause of the greater condemnation.

Any who will begin to live even the very first part of that first and great commandment will be able to contact that divine Light of Christ. And no man can possibly have a special claim to It or a monopoly upon It for It is given to abide in every man who cometh into the world. Only as one fulfills the law of laws and learns to love with *all* his heart can he release that Christ Light into his life. As one begins to learn to *love with all his heart* his life begins to conform to the higher law because he will be *living* it. Those who refuse to *live* Christ's revealed, higher laws will continue to walk in their own darkness at noonday. Such will remain blind and to counteract their blindness they may preach a little louder and become a little more strident and fanatical in their arguments as they seek to justify their empty beliefs, not realizing that His Kingdom is not in *words,* but in *power!*

As one loves God with all his soul every cell, atom, sinew, nerve, organ and fiber of his being will be filled with that love and the expanding, released, glorified Light of Christ. In that great love and the dynamic, outflowing Christ Light, the seed of himself, the man God intended the individual to become, will be quickened and made alive. As that spiritual being is brought forth the physical body is quickened and renewed—even exalted. In this developing process the physical body will be transformed, transfigured and translated into a new being. And this is Life Eternal. This is the power that overcomes death.

As one loves God with all his mind the great blindness of mind will be removed and he will have the power and vision to fully behold the glory of God and his eyes will "become single to that glory"! In this love all the evil, ugly thoughts of darkness, dismay, hate, jealousy, lust, greed and fear are converted and the Light of Christ fills the mind with Its quickening, enlightening, ineffable, revealing beauty as one begins to comprehend all things. With the mind thus purified and enlightened one will think only the most glorious, beautiful, divinely powerful thoughts possible. And in that glorious power of such thinking and such vision his thoughts will be lifted to the very heights of heaven and he will take on the glory of all that his vision beholds. For "The land thou seest will I give unto thee."

When one's mind is thus purified by love and enlightened by the Light of Christ the conscious mind and the great super-conscious mind become as ONE—blended in the glory of Christ's Light of noonday brilliance. In this state of at-one-ment that inner spiritual being is brought forth from the seed of God, contained within the individual, and the very powers of God are released into action in the life of man.

As one loves God with all his strength, the body, mind and soul become unified and coordinated as they take on the qualities of the Spirit. Man himself becomes a dynamoed, energized Spiritual generator as he fulfills that first and greatest of all commandments.

And man himself is the recipient of the glory of the fulfilling of the most powerful and wonderful of all laws. And it is man who is the real benefactor, for it is man who is glorified by such love and such fulfilling.

It is in this fulfilled law of love that one sheds his mortal status and his darkness or blindness and steps forth into the Light of divinity—or noonday.

Then, *as one loves his neighbor as himself*, he learns to look into his brother's soul in tender, understanding compassion. He no longer condemns that brother for what he is or is not, for his blindness or what appears on the outside. One no longer dislikes anyone for what he does or does not do. He loves him for that Seed of Perfection and for that Light of Christ which is implanted in his soul. He loves him for what he was intended to become—and in that love he helps his brother to become THAT! He no longer condemns any man for being either ignorant or blind. He loves him even as he loves himself and possibly more.

As this great love is developed it becomes impossible to look at any without beholding the divine workmanship of the Creator. And with this love-awakened vision he beholds all things through the eyes of revealing glory. He exults in all creation as he enjoys more fully the perfection of a blue sky, the whisper of a breeze, the rustling of leaves, the song of birds, the breathtaking wonder and beauty of a rose. Then lifting his love-filled eyes to heaven, he realizes that no rose is as perfect and glorious or as divinely fashioned and powerful as is man. Man is God's great masterpiece! Man is indeed the very offspring of God as God's seed of immaculate conception is fulfilled in him. When one comprehends the great glory of God as it is contained and implanted within man, he stands breathlessly awed in humbled reverence and love-filled wonder.

This great love begins to expand as wide as eternity while it reaches out to enfold the race of men. And as it wings its way out on Christ's holy, released Light it carries healing and glory with it.

This love is the great God-like love as it becomes active in the lives of men.

This is the love which contains all the powers of complete forgiveness for in this love is manifested only forgiving compassion and divine understanding. This is the love which fulfills perfection as one begins to see as God sees and to think as God thinks—and to feel as God feels. In this love one could not possibly cheat, steal, harm, injure or transgress against his brother. He cannot injure by either thought, word or act. "This is the point where one's mind and lips have lost the power to hurt and wound and from thenceforth his voice is heard among the Gods."

Within these two great commandments is contained the power and the Light of the Ages. Within these laws is contained man's membership in the Church and Kingdom of the Firstborn, even the Son of God, and with the Assembly of the Brotherhood of Light. The great Brotherhood of Light is composed of those who contacted and brought forth that divine Light of Christ right within themselves, while still in the flesh. These are the ones who by that Light comprehended all things, hence overcame all things— even death.

Fulfill these laws and it will not matter in the least whether you are sprinkled or immersed; whether you give contributions or pay tithing; partake of the sacrament or attend confession; give your life to attending orthodox meetings of earthly conformity, or even your talents and entire strength and existence to some service, or your body to be burned—which services are often empty, meaningless often harmful services. For all laws are completely fulfilled in the two great eternal laws of LOVE! In these great laws only can one serve as he is directed by God Himself. These two great laws not only fulfill all other laws, they lift the individual who fulfills them into a higher vibration, or dimension.

This is what Christ meant when the woman of Samaria said, "Our fathers worshipped in this mountain; and ye say, that in Jerusalem is the place to worship.

"And Jesus saith unto her, Woman, believe me, the hour cometh, when ye shall neither in this mountain, nor yet at Jerusalem, worship the Father—For the hour cometh, and now is, when the true worshippers shall worship the Father in *Spirit* and in truth: for the Father seeketh such to worship him."

He who worships in Spirit and in truth will worship with his whole being, his mind, his body and his soul— and in this reverence the great law of love will be fulfilled in all its released power of completing glory. It is in this type of worship that all laws will be glorified and perfected and all love be released in praise and gratitude and singing glory as one becomes filled with the very *"Fullness of God"!*

"And all things will become subject unto such a one, both in heaven and on earth, the life and the light, the Spirit and the power, sent forth by the Will of the Father, through Jesus Christ, His Son." These are the promises and these are the laws which govern them.

In this true form of worship and fulfilled love none can possibly walk in darkness. In these fulfilled laws and released life-giving powers the brilliance of the noonday Light is apparent and one is given the power to Behold His glory! And as man's eyes become single to that glory it must also begin to be fulfilled in him.

Those who are walking in the darkness of their own blindness are the unenlightened ones who know not the powers of the great Christ Light which is contained right within themselves. They are rejecting that Light and are hence remaining under condemnation. They know nothing of that divine seed of God which lies dormant and unfulfilled within that Light. Those who *live* the laws *know* of their power and their fulfilling glory.

Behold! The Light of noonday! The Light of Christ, the Lord! Rejoice in that Light and learn to walk therein! Glorify God and give praise and honor to Him continually for the miracle and the wonder of "This great Christ Light that has been given to abide in you" and you will become glorious!

THE DOOR BETWEEN THE TWO WORLDS

Chapter XIX

There is a door through which man passes almost constantly back and forth between two realms, the spiritual and the mortal. That door has two sides and those sides are as different as the realms into which they lead.

The side of the door which opens from the mortal, physical existence is almost intangible it is so delicately wrought. It is not discernible to the flesh senses at all. It becomes discernible only through comprehension, for it is spiritual. It is the door through which one steps into a higher vibratory field or realm of existence as spiritual thoughts and deep reverence fill his being. It could be called the door of prayer, but only when prayer is exalted into a triumphant song of praise and loving gratitude. As this type of prayer is developed the pure Christ Light is contacted and that door swings open. And though one may not be fully aware of it, he is in a higher vibratory state of existence. He has entered the realm of Spirit.

This chapter is written that man may comprehend fully the door by which he entered the higher realm and that he may also learn to maintain his place there permanently that he "go no more out".

This higher spiritual realm is the one in which all the divine powers of God are released into complete activity to fulfill the noble desires and aspiration of the soul.

275

In order to comprehend the spiritual realm into which that door leads it must first be necessary to reveal the door clearly so that all who desire may enter.

All who have been inspired by true devotion have stepped back and forth through that door. Without complete understanding however they invariably return to the lower vibrational plane of mortal existence. Those who now desire to comprehend that door will be able to look and behold it clearly. They can also have the power to lock that door behind them if they so desire, so they need never return to the grubby mortal, vibrational realm. There is only one thing that must be definitely understood and that is that it is impossible to serve two masters or reside simultaneously within both realms. Those who reside in the higher vibrational realm of peace and achievement and divine glory must make the choice and in doing so close that door behind them so they will never more return to the mortal plane of "outer darkness" with its inherent evils, dismays, distresses, suffering and death.

Man can, by his own understanding, not only close that door behind him but he can lock it so securely no vibration of earth's negation and evil can possibly touch him. This can be accomplished as soon as man opens his eyes to behold the contrast between the material, mortal realm of evil and the wondrous glory of the realm of Light.

At first one may enter that higher vibrational realm without realizing just how or even why it happened. And until he understands the difference between the two realms and is able to master that door he usually fluctuates back and forth between the two kingdoms, for they *are* definite kingdoms. One is of joy and happiness and peace and power, the other is of fears, worries, distress and darkness. It is quite possible for man to ascend into the realm of Light on the wings of ecstasy and descend again into the realms of darkest mortal despondency without comprehending in the least what caused the transition.

It is time man realizes that that door belongs to himself. Its two sides are the two sides of his own nature—the spiritual and the physical.

From the side of Light the door is camouflaged. It is an exit so subtly concealed one scarcely realizes he has been drawn back through it until he finds himself sitting for-lornly upon the grubby earth. Man has not realized that he himself opened up that door and hence ejected himself back through the opening into a discordant world. One always leaves that higher realm, where he may have gained entrance for a brief span, through the opening of his old thought patterns of negation, fear, dislikes, dismays, dis-cordant or selfish thinking, his old worthless memories and any type of mortal lusts or perversions. It is impossible for these negative things or thoughts to remain upon that higher spiritual plane and he who reaches back for such possess-ions will have to return to the realm in which they belong. As one opens his mind to any of his habitual thought pat-terns of mortal concepts or earthly thinking, he will find himself back on the mortal plane of existence and that ex-alted experience which lifted him triumphantly into the Light becomes only a lingering memory. It may be quickly forgotten and it is possible that realm may have been en-tered only once or twice in one's entire lifetime, depend-ing on the individual and often on his devotional back-ground.

But whether a man is a great spiritual leader or just a common layman he may fluctuate between those two realms without laying claim to the higher glory unless he fully comprehends the issues involved and becomes the master of that door. He may arise upon the clouds of joyous ecstasy and then again descend into the dark, desolate misery of the lowest depths of despair.

So it is that this door must be comprehended fully and mastered if one desires to remain permanently within the realms of Light.

This chapter has been written for those of you who desire to reach beyond drab earthly, mortal living. To you I shall seek to reveal the door and show you how to seal it behind you as you step through it into the glory of eternal Light. You must comprehend the reality of that door and open it knowingly and with complete awareness if you are to pass permanently into the higher realm. To you who can lift your vision and your desires to attain unto the heigths, the drab existence of earthly vibrational decadence and darkness can become a forgotten state and be left behind as completely as one steps from his soiled, worn-out garments.

To step through this door is every man's heritage. So it is that "He who prays continually, without ceasing, becomes filled with Light and comprehends all things", for he is no longer abiding in the darkness but is abiding in the Light. And so it is, that "He who is thankful in all things shall be made glorious", for he has evolved into the vibrational realm of glory and the darkness of earth is left behind.

This door, which is the entrance into the higher vibrational realm of Light, is the front door into the other world. It is the door that by-passes the back door of death. And you, blessed one, have stepped across that threshold many times during your sojourn on earth, have returned to abide upon the mortal plane simply because you did not know how to hold your place in the realms of Light.

It is now time that you understand so you may fully comprehend the door and the two realms it links together. This is the door at which Christ is knocking and you must open that door knowingly and with complete understanding. As you open it with full awareness you will have achieved the status of what you were intended to become and will have the power to remain within the realms of Light, if so be you choose. And you will choose to remain permanently in the higher vibrational plane of spiritual advancement, for the change is as extreme and the joy as great as, greater than that experienced by a blind man who suddenly receives his sight. The old world of darkness is left behind and henceforth you will abide in the world of eternal Light.

It is true that one may travel back and forth many times until he advances far enough to comprehend fully that door and realizes he has the key to it. It is as he uses that key to lock the door behind him that secures his position in the higher realms.

Christ said, "I am the door: by me if any man enter in, he shall be saved, and shall go in and out and find pastures." (John 10:9) As the Light of Christ is first contacted one gains entrance into that higher realm and is *saved*, or salvaged. He can also go in and out and find his moments or periods of spiritual pasturing. But after he comprehends fully he passes beyond the condition of being merely *saved*. He becomes *exalted*, elevated into a higher condition. Such a one need no longer "go in and out". He may remain permanently.

"Him that overcometh (that door) will I make a pillar

in the temple of my God, and *he shall go no more out*: and I will write upon him the name of my God, and the name of the city of my God, which is new Jerusalem, which cometh down out of heaven from my God: and I will write upon him my new name." (Rev. 3:12)

That door is as real as any door in existence. It is intangible to the physical senses because it is spiritual. It is a door in consciousness.

In the instant you comprehend the door and exert your ability to open it by your own power of higher thinking, your transition is established.

That door is but the opening of your own being to the glory of the great Christ Light, through love and praise and singing gratitude—the greatest attitude. The divine, inner song of loving adoration opens the door into the higher, vibrational realm of existence. To become established permanently in the higher realm and to hold your place in it requires only that as you enter into that realm you close the door behind you. You must close it against every mortal thought and every earthly concept and every shadow of negation and doubt. It is your privilege to step out fearlessly into the Light and to remain in the divine, higher vibrational plane permanently. As you do so you are treading the glorified road Christ traveled, the road of Eternal Life.

In order to step through that door and to hold your place in the realms of Light, it is only necessary to lift your own vibrations. The law of eternity and of existence is that all things must abide within the vibrational sphere of their own degree of development. Any person who can lift himself into a higher thought vibration must step into the higher vibrational level of his own thought action. Man alone is given the power to so exalt his own vibrations through higher thought action so he can be lifted into continually higher vibrational levels of Spiritual advancement. This is quite possible even while he is still clothed in flesh. In fact, his own flesh, when lifted by the Spiritual vibrations of glory, can exalt him more completely and more speedily than any other condition in existence possibly could. If man can lift his flesh in this exalting way into a spiritual texture, he has achieved the great step, has entered through that great Front Door into the realms of glory without needing to die.

The transition is most easily achieved by praising God continually. Rejoice without ceasing. Keep your eyes single to the glory of God and bask in that glory. Praise constantly and give joyous thanksgiving. The door of death will be closed and you will have power to step forward into the realms of Eternal Light.

As you learn to hold your place within the realms of Light, soon, very soon, your vision will be extended to encompass the spiritual realm you have entered and its powers of fulfilling glory will be yours to use. You will automatically advance into the powers of God.

As you step through that door do not hesitate or look back. The strongest pull back into the darkness is always at the entrance, or just within the door. It takes great effort and determination to close it securely behind you. It is most easily accomplished by keeping your eyes lifted to the glory of God, to the thrilling ecstasy of the vibrations and reality of the enfolding Light and with increasing praise and love. Step forth boldly into the Light. You need not grovel, my dearly beloved one, for this is your heritage. It is waiting for you to enter—and the time is NOW!

All that is necessary to fulfill the great, divine law of believing is that you "be-living" according to your own request or desire every moment of your life. If you do this it must be fulfilled unto you! This is the law!

Only know that in using this unfailing, irrevocable law of infinite power, if your desire is not for the good of all, or if any living soul would be injured by it, then know that it will bring your own injury and perhaps your own destruction. The law is divine and must be used according to the laws of divinity—fulfilling the eternal, universal law of *love*.

When the Russian nation re-crucified Christ and cast God and His laws from its land and from its heart it only shut Him and His divine love and powers out from itself. When this greatest tragedy the world ever witnessed took place one great and noble Russian lady could not join in the debauchery of Divinity and in anguished heart pleaded, "Oh dear God, please let me *know* if You exist! I must *know*, dear God! I *must* know!"

In answer to her soul query and her intense, yearning prayer she received the answer of the Almighty as it permeated her entire being from the crown of her head to the soles of her feet and filled the air around her, "Daughter, *live* as though I were and you shall *know* that I Am!"

All that is required to fulfill any holy request is that you be-living every moment of your life according to the desire of your soul and the holy, unfailing law of believing will be fulfilled unto you.

Know also that whatsoever you desire to *be* that is pure and noble and beautiful, you will *Be Come!* All that is necessary is that you live true to your desire in thought, word and act. Live true to your ideal, your request, your inner desire and you will *be* it! Come! Step into the usage of this higher law. This is true righteousness. This *is* the "right-use" of the eternal laws of our Almighty Father of glory and love and fulfillment.

Beloved, Be! Come and fulfill the law of *knowing* and of receiving and of power. The law cannot fail! It is irrevocable, eternal, unfailing and all-powerful! To *become* anything you desire you must BE! COME!

Always the invitation to *be* and to *come* is waiting for you. Your part is to be-living according to your request.

"Know the Truth and the Truth shall make you free" as you live in accordance with It.

Know that whatever you desire to be you can BE! COME! Come, beloved! Come! The doors of a new age, a new dispensation and a higher realm of existence are open to you NOW! Come! Just Be and Come!

Come, you radiant sons of God! Be your own divine selves! Come and Be!

Come, you glorious daughters of God! Come! Array yourselves in the garments of holiness as you clothe yourselves in Light.

Learn to hold out the original plan of yourself, in all the glorified perfection with which God endowed it and watch that perfection take form. It must *be* for it already *is!* This is the you God created! It must *be! Come!*

If you will only *be-living* according to the deep inner anointing it must *be!* Come! Come! Watch the unfolding of yourself, the growth and fulfillment of yourself as you *become* that which you already *are!* This divine, glorious you is the one God created! This beautiful, breathtaking you is the one He is holding in His plan. In His will is only the yearning desire that you BE COME It! This magnificent, glorious you is the one He created you to BE! COME! Fill the measure of your creation, the pattern of your own being, for this IS you!

The keys of your own glory are hereby placed in your hands—the keys of the Millennium—the keys of the New Age. These are the mysteries of eternity. I hand them over to you—NOW!

The Beatitudes are only the admonition to BE that attitude of meekness, to be a peacemaker or to be any attitude whatsoever and you will BE COME or receive whatever law you fulfill. *Be-living* according to your requests or desires as though you had already received, for this is how all doubts are banished, so you will never "Doubt in your heart and you shall have whatsoever you saith". *Be-living* it every moment of your life and you will have not only proved your faith of believing, you will have fulfilled the law upon which all requests are granted and fulfilled.

————

I leave the way Christ traveled, re-marked and clarified. It is unmistakable for it is lighted by His Own Glory and with His divine Light. In this Light the road of hope and vision *becomes* the glorified highway of one's own perfected fulfillment, according to His plan. It is the highway paved with transparent gold as the holy feet of His advancing children tread upon it in their upward march.

So I have been permitted to write. And so it is written.

This record is henceforth your own. It came forth according to the WILL of God, for His glory and for your exaltation. God be with you, my dearly beloved, in your fulfilling of it as you *be come!* "Yea, come! And drink of the waters of life freely!"

So be it! Amen!

THE ANCIENT PATH RECLAIMED!

Up perpendicular ledges and towering granite cliffs
We've snatched at jutting projections and clung to cloud-
wrapped rifts!
Souls despairing in anguish, we've struggled in hopeless
dismay,
Seeking His trail to follow as we've climbed our rugged way!
Never were craigs so awesome! Nor ever a mountain so
steep!
Nor ever a need so urgent a rendezvous to keep!
Of't with torn, bleeding bodies we've clung to some swaying
ledge,
Or only held on blindly to some crumbling, precarious edge!
We've snatched at roots or gravel to feel them give way at
our touch!
We've asked so very little! And needed that "little" so much!
Once, hurled back by a landslide, we lay bruised against a
tree,
While above, on the top of that mountain, awaited a destiny!
A thousand times we were hurled back in a broken,
anguished heap!
A thousand pit-falls overcome, our rendezvous to keep!
A million hazardous testings we faced in that upward climb!
A million sobbing heartbreaks, etched deep on the face of
"time"!
The top of the mountain was cloud-banked, the goal obscure,
unclear—

It was only a dream, seen vaguely, as we climbed those
  crags in fear!

'Twas only a vision beckoned, above the dreary world—

Only a vision of glory that ever its promise unfurled!

At last! Aft'r years of struggle! A seeming eternity!

Our goal loomed high above us! Our rendezvoused destiny!

Inch by inch! Slowly! Soul-searing! We grappled with
  elements wild!

Exiled! Cast out in discredit like destiny's orphaned child!

So many times, on that last cliff, we were hurled to the
  ledge below!

But somewhere along that upward climb our "faith" had
  advanced to "KNOW"!

Up that ledge we dug our way! Up! Up the mountain so
  steep!

Up! Up through those exiled years of life, our destiny to
  keep!

Our strength increased with our progress! Joy became
  mighty and strong!

In danger, or heart-rending setbacks, we'd lift up our hearts
  in song!

When we'd finally reached the top, place of our noble,
  destined tryst,

We breathed in humbled, breathless awe as we kneeled at
  the feet of Christ!

"You've traveled the road I mapped for man, the way to
  overcome!

You've learned to hear the voice of God! And let his will
  be done!

The road I left the map for, that age-dimmed, forgotten Way

You have blazed anew in power more brilliant than the day!

Turn! And look back where you've traveled! Look back
where the mountain has been!

There's my open highway of glory you've rebuilt for the
race of men!"

Breinigsville, PA USA
17 November 2010
249524BV00002B/205/A